Dark Psychology 101 2021:

Understanding the Techniques of Covert Manipulation, Mind Control, Influence, and Persuasion

By Moneta Raye

Table of Contents

Introduction

Congratulations on purchasing *Dark Psychology 101*, and thank you for doing so.

The following chapters will discuss all the major topics related to dark psychology. You will first learn about the key concepts and definitions involved when we talk about dark psychology before jumping into specific techniques, tools, and strategies used by many different types of people worldwide. The people who practice dark psychology are as varied and unique as the strategies themselves. While some practitioners spend hours, days, or years of their lives studying the psychology behind these practices, some people develop a natural "talent" for things like manipulation and mind games because they've learned that people can be easy prey once they realize the commonalities of human psychology and how to exploit the more influential aspects of the human character and traits like empathy, sociability, kindness, and gullibility. These traits would be considered positive and signals of a good person in a normal working society. Think of the young girl on her way to school who is everyone's friend and offers her time to charity and extracurricular work. The person who offers help to complete strangers when they ask for it has not experienced the darker sides of humanity.

But for the manipulator, these personality traits don't just signal someone who might give them a helping hand in whatever situation. They see someone they can use to their advantage through dark psychology techniques and practices. We call these people predators, criminals, and scam artists; the list goes on. So while a kind, trusting person is a great thing, there is still the reality to acknowledge that there are less favorable people out there constantly on the lookout for personalities that can be easily manipulated.

In this book, you'll be introduced to what exactly dark psychology is and how to recognize it. You'll learn how important it is to be aware when these strategies may be used on you or someone you know or care about. In chapter 2, we'll discuss the startling prevalence of practitioners of dark psychology, as well as where these people are often found in modern day society. Where do they operate? What do they look for? How successful are they in different arenas?

In the next chapter, you'll learn how to recognize when someone is using dark psychology techniques on you and how to spot it when it's happening, as well as how to derail the person's efforts before they get something from you that you didn't even know you were offering. These lessons can be life-saving, so pay attention to the tips and tricks in this chapter.

In chapter 4, we'll talk about some specific techniques used in manipulation by looking at a few examples of these practitioners in action. You'll learn specific terminology used to refer to these techniques, and we will illustrate a complete scene where those strategies may be used. In all likelihood, you've been present in a situation in which someone was trying to manipulate someone nearby. Public places like bars and even coffee shops can be a hunting ground for those looking for the perfect opportunity to "meet" someone new to prime them for manipulation.

In the next chapter, we'll discuss mind control in particular. We'll define terms and tools like gaslighting and discuss how incredibly damaging these experiences can be for victims.

Chapter 6 is all about how dark psychology is used specifically to seduce and gain the trust of someone they hope to exploit sexually or emotionally. There are many different angles and degrees to which these practices are applied and practiced. We are talking about both the young man who lies and showers compliments to get a girl to come home with him, as well as the latest serial killer looking to gain the affection or pity of a naïve girl just long enough to get her in his car.

The Dark Triad is the topic of chapter 7, which includes the three-pronged collection of personalities that are most often associated with the practice of dark psychology. They are the narcissist, the sociopath, and the Machiavellian personality types. You will learn what differentiates these three types, as well as how they are similar. By the end of this chapter, you will have learned several tips on how to spot someone who falls into one of these categories.

In chapter 8, we'll discuss the art of deception and the mind games that often accompany them. Deception is a broad term and includes such innocent practices as a magician using sleight of hand to convince an audience that something is happening when it really isn't. It extends to the tricky tactics used by false mystics and mediums in a time when Harry Houdini traveled all over the place to catch these scam artists in the act as they tricked grieving widows out of their money.

We'll move on then to discuss the specifics of brainwashing, how it is done, who is vulnerable, and how to shut it down if you think someone is trying to use this technique on you or someone you know.

In chapter 10, we'll switch gears to discuss the importance of body language and how we all communicate using nonverbal communication. We will discuss micro-expressions and how to read another person or get them to like you quickly. These techniques are used by people all over the world. Some of these practitioners include people trying to climb the ladder at work by getting "in" with their superiors.

Finally, in chapter 11, we'll focus on best practices for defense against practitioners who routinely put these dark psychology strategies into practice. You've likely been a target in your lifetime, even if you have no idea what was going on. Perhaps the person was unsuccessful, or perhaps they were, but you didn't realize what had happened until it's too late. Some of you may be reading this book precisely because you have been a victim in the past, and you want to learn to protect yourself and recognize it when someone tries these tools on you again. Whatever your reason is for reading Dark Psychology, by the end of chapter 11, you will have given yourself some very important lessons regarding self-preservation and defense against the dark psychology arsenal.

There are plenty of books on this subject on the market, so thanks again for choosing this one! Every effort was made to ensure it is full of as much useful information as possible. Please enjoy!

Chapter 1: What Is Dark Psychology?

Dark Psychology is at once a simple and quite complex topic. It encompasses the ways in which one person gets something from another person without them being aware of their tactics or the motivation behind those tactics. Many practitioners become quite skilled at hiding ulterior motives. They put on a mask that conveys to people that their feelings or intent is straightforward when, in fact, they are anything but.

This is why we call the subject of dark psychology. The victim of dark psychology is most likely in the dark about what is happening to them, and the victim may never find out, or they may only figure things out when it is too late, or the perpetrator has moved on. Now, it is important to note that not all forms of dark psychology are inherently malicious. As mentioned in the introduction to this book, dark psychology includes things like sleight of hand in a magic show, which is used to entertain an audience. However, a skilled pickpocket can also use sleight of hand who roams around crowded tourist areas, stealing money and other easily accessible items. TThe key distinction is that the person on whom these practices are being applied does not know that this particular strategy is being used. As viewers, we may know that a magician is simply using a trick to convince us that something has disappeared, but we don't necessarily know the mechanism of that trick, even when we realize that we were fooled. Again, this is a lighthearted and entertaining application of dark psychology, but the kind we'll be discussing in this book is on the much darker and more malicious side of the spectrum.

Why is it important to learn about dark psychology? People decide to educate themselves on the strategies and tools of dark psychology for different reasons. Some may actually like to learn a few tricks of the trade in order to get ahead in some aspect of their lives, while others want to learn how to detect predators and steer clear of those who might seek to manipulate them. Whatever your reasons for picking up this book, you will indeed find that you are much more educated and prepared to engage with the concepts of dark psychology once you've completed this reading.

The only way to constructively discuss the origins of dark psychology is to discuss each topic individually. This is because, as stated earlier, dark psychology covers a vast amount of territory. It is certain that the most elementary and instinctive forms have existed in human society since organized society itself has been in existence. People rose to the top of the food chain and, over time, developed a system for recognizing the leaders or alphas to whom others would submit. This primitive hierarchy is still followed today in many social circles. For example, the group of high school boys who like to hang out at the mall might have one person in their group who is the most good-looking, the most athletic, the most charismatic, or even all three at once. When the group notices an attractive young girl, there is often an unspoken understanding that the alpha, or leader, gets first dibs. This is because no one else in the group is willing or capable of fighting the alpha with the intent to take his place. These things work almost without our active consciousness as a natural way to organize and make sense of ourselves as organizations of society. The same kind of thing happens at work, in school, in political office, etc.

Dark psychology comes into play in these areas of elementary social hierarchy when individuals use covert or manipulative behaviors in order to establish themselves higher up in that hierarchy. They may lie, cheat, or steal in order to establish their dominance and capability. Again, these behaviors are as old as human organized society itself, and their applications and variances are too numerable to count.

However, dark psychology has also integrated several different areas of specialization and research, which have been established and pursued to understand human behavior, psychology, and, finally, criminality. We know that human beings do not always interact with each other in totally benevolent ways, and the deviant human beings in our society are the ones causing the most harm and damage. Some researchers come to the discipline out of sheer interest and fascination, while other entities, like law enforcement, are obsessed with figuring out exactly what makes someone like the narcissistic serial killer tick. If

they can unlock what is going on in these criminals'
minds and understand their tactics, it would
give them a leg up on their investigations. The
problem is, as the very nature of these tactics is
"dark," it is very difficult to detect the workings of
a criminal narcissist of sociopath until the damage is done and the victims come
forward or, in the worst cases, bodies are recovered.

And, dark psychology does not solely exist in the realm of criminals. Especially in
recent years, illegal and coercive interrogation tactics have come to light through
major news outlets, documentaries, new evidence, and TV shows, which highlight
the reality that sometimes, even the "good guys" will go to desperate measures to
get what they want or maintain the reputations of their law enforcement
organizations. False confessions leading to years or even life in prison are utilized
in court and are sometimes proven false once the real culprits are caught. But
sometimes, the guilty get away with their crimes when the incorrect person is
blamed and convicted. Unfortunately, many of these cases reflect flagrant racism
and laziness on the part of a few law enforcement officials. And, while there are
thousands of skilled, honest officers and investigators working in modern society,
extreme cases lead to grossly negative outcomes, which always make the front
page.

The sensationalism and true crime popularity frenzy are partially to blame for a
reignited interest in dark psychology by those who do not work in realms like law

enforcement. Now, it feels increasingly important to be able to defend and rely on yourself in these situations where dark psychology is used maliciously. It may be statistically unlikely that you are going to come face to face with a manipulative serial killer or a sociopathic, gaslighting boyfriend, but you certainly would want to have been prepared in the case where you hit on that narrow likelihood, wouldn't you?

This is why I can't say that reporting, social media, a renewed interest in true crime, corruption in the law enforcement arena, and dark psychology are altogether unfortunate evolution in the age of personal responsibility. As our cities get bigger, and political and social unrest grow in intensity, the hunting grounds ripe with potential targets become larger and closer together. There is no downside to taking it upon yourself to become educated and more aware of the potential threats in modern society.

With that said, there is another facet to dark psychology that we will explore that has a lot more to do with active observation and positive psychology and a lot less to do with serial killers.

Neuro-linguistic programming and other facets of psychology research focus on reprogramming your brain to perform better or differently as a way to relieve negative disorders that affect people's lives, such as depression and anxiety. NLP, in particular, is used in many situations by people who seek to teach their brains to reinterpret those triggers which have always prompted negative feelings. These harmful mental experiences can often lead to lifelong struggles of becoming productive and fulfilled. And this may lead to isolation, loneliness, perceived failures, and often, a deepening of those underlying mood disorders. NLP is one way to help a person retrain their brains in those moments when it really counts. This strategy, developed in the 70s, utilizes the brain's relationship to language and how it interprets language and information in everyday life. It teaches the brain through repetition and consistent application to replace those feelings of anxiety, fear, self-doubt, etc., with more positive and constructive emotional and behavioral reactions. The research and application of NLP have improved many people's lives, and, in particular, it has been useful in treating those mental states which arise from a particular trauma or past experience with an emotional manipulator.

The Dark Triad personalities date back much further and encompass the realm of the narcissist, the sociopath, and the Machiavellian types. While these personalities themselves have existed in human beings for probably as long as we've been organizing into societies, the actual focus on research and understanding in terms of psychology is much more recent. It was recognized that it is not just important to be able to identify these individuals in society. We also need to have some basis of understanding in order to combat and prevent the potential harm inflicted on these people's targets.

While many forms of dark psychology can be used on an organizational level, such as illegal interrogation tactics and organized crime, the tactics utilized on a personal, often one-on-one, level are some of the most interesting and malicious examples of dark psychology in practice today. The reason the Dark Triad is so closely associated with dark psychology is that these strategies are very often integrated and applied in their lives, almost like a natural talent. Their skills arise out of necessity and drive to acquire what they want from other people, but they have to devise manipulative tactics because they do not have the capacity or willingness to acquire them in acceptable ways. While the different personalities differ in key ways, one of the commonalities is that they are all willing to hurt other people in order to get what they want with little or no empathy involved. Because of the very nature of their willingness and coldness when it comes to other people, dark psychology tactics are a natural progression, as they often teach themselves as they identify their proclivities and natural talents.

But, you don't have to be a narcissist to be tempted to utilize dark psychology methods on others, even loved ones. And, sometimes, when personal motivations and desires are strong, we can all be susceptible to taking action and saying things that we regret later on. We have lied in order to make ourselves appear more attractive or more skilled, even if they were just "white" lies. This is a facet of dark psychology—you are leading someone to believe something that is not altogether true about you in order to achieve your desired result or impression. As I've said, the spectrum of use and application of dark psychology is a wide range and encompasses behaviors from the most benign white lie to the most sadistic mind games. It's important to realize this because people can fall back on dark psychology even without a history of malicious intent. When people become desperate or consumed by a desired outcome or goal, and none of the standard accepted ways of getting there are working, people can get a little devious in their methods. For example, in one of our chapters, we discuss seduction and the dark psychology that may be involved in a man trying to get a woman to come home with him or a similar scenario. When a man realizes that he lacks in one important area when it comes to social skills or relatability to women, he might employ dark psychology tactics simply because he sees no other feasible way to get what he wants. Some of these guys try their hand at lying to make themselves look good or flattery or some other tactic and fail miserably. Others learn to observe and learn about their targets before actually making their first moves. We will discuss in detail how the preparation phase of observation plays a key role in the successful outcome of dark psychology tactics as we move through this book.

Finally, I want to briefly discuss one of the less often acknowledged realities of dark psychology. That is the fact that everyone harbors an innate susceptibility and proclivity for both utilizing and falling prey to these tactics, whether you feel invulnerable and hyper-aware or not. Some very intelligent people have fallen prey to cult recruiters and are lucky enough to be able to share their experiences after the dark practices of the cult are revealed. People have an incredible capacity to practice denial when something they value or the realities they are comfortable with are threatened. It's the phenomenon where people refuse to believe something they don't want to believe, even if the overwhelming evidence is staring them in the face.

You have probably heard of some of the most famous psychology experiments from the 70s in which the darker sides of human nature were revealed. One of them involved taking volunteers and putting them in a situation where they were expected to inflict pain on another human being for the sake of science. The results were quite astounding and surprising. The experiment is referred to as the Milgram Experiment and originated from a man named Dr. Stanley Milgram, a psychologist at Yale University in 1961.

The experiment was controversial, not just because of the results but because of how the experiment was conducted. Volunteers were brought in and introduced to someone they thought was another volunteer but actually part of the experimenters' team. This person was required to employ a bit of acting skill. It was explained that this person would be hooked up to a machine on the other side of a wall—literally strapped and unable to move—while the volunteer would be operating the machine, which would inflict progressive intensities of brief electric shocks. The volunteer was asked to read off a series of questions to the man strapped to the chair. Each time the man answered incorrectly, the volunteer was instructed to press the button, which would engage the electric shock. The voltage would increase as the man strapped to the machine answered more and more questions incorrectly. TThe experiment aimed to see how far people would go when they were pressured to follow instructions by an authority figure. The results might surprise you. No less than two-thirds of the experiment's participants progressed all the way to the infliction of a lethal level of electronic shock at 450 volts. And all of the participants were willing to progress up to 300.

The experiment was conducted shortly after the trial of a Nazi named Adolf Eichmann, and Milgram wanted to look more closely at this question regarding the Nazi's defense that he was "just following orders." How was it possible that seemingly benevolent and intelligent human beings could be convinced to engage in unethical practices toward others? The answers and theories arising from this question go beyond the scope of this book, but my point is that factors of which many of us are unaware can play a role in whether or not we fall victim to manipulative or coercive behaviors. When we deem an authority figure to know what they are doing and choose to place our trust in him, it becomes easier to get past certain levels of doubt and even pangs of warning coming from our conscience because we have formed a paradigm in our minds that associates only benevolent and trustworthy characteristics and intentions with this figure. There is also the element of peer pressure and the universal desire to not stick out in the crowd or be the one who is "different." This is an elementary facet of evolutionary instinct designed to support the social nature essential to human survival. When the Nazis donned those identical uniforms and associated themselves with an overarching philosophy that supported the success of their country, coupled with a charismatic speaker and leader in whom they learned to place their trust, those individuals soon found themselves in an environment where it became rather easy to overlook the unethical nature of their actions simply because of the sense of a greater purpose. Also, as part of a group, any blame and guilt they may have faced could be easily associated and placed on the group rather than the individual.

All of this is to say that none of us are exempted from the seduction of dark psychology. We all have desires and needs and aspirations, and sometimes, it is tempting to take the short cut when it comes to utilizing other people to our ends. The focus of this book is to open the door to awareness and understanding where these dark psychology strategies are concerned and open your eyes to the fact that the dark psychology practitioner does not always look the part. Even those whom you've trusted and loved for years can turn on you in the worst circumstances and use your love against you. This is the scary and tragic reality of dark psychology and one which you will master as you read on.

Chapter 2: How Prevalent Is Dark Psychology?

Now that we've discussed a bit about the different types of dark psychology which exist in society, we will now demonstrate how prevalent these practices really are in modern-day society. Because our idea of the dark psychology practitioner cannot be limited to obviously deviant or those with clear criminal intent, the array of environments in which potential victims live out their day-to-day lives expands to include even those locations which might not be the first considered. We can imagine the dark alleyway or even a crowded bar as great hunting grounds for the predator employing dark psychology tactics, but oftentimes, our first encounters with dark psychology occur a little closer to home—inside the home, to be exact.

What we experience in our childhood often has a profound effect on how we turn out as human beings—what our values and morals are, how that reflects whatever religious or spiritual practices we were brought up around, how we treat and respect others, and whether or not we are taught to be afraid of or dislike those who are different from us—the list goes on and on. Though, we don't always turn out exactly as our parents had intended. Sometimes, this is a disappointment; other times, people break out of the antiquated, immoral practices or ways of thinking of their parents to become better, more informed people. These experiences can be rather benign and might include things like realizing as a teenager that you do not share the religious values your parents have taught you or the political views. Perhaps your parents wanted you to go to school and follow in their footsteps in terms of a career, but you soon discovered you didn't enjoy their occupation.

Sometimes, however, people experience hurtful behavior, verbal abuse, or both, which, over time, distorts their perception of how people should interact with one another. If, for example, a young boy was taught throughout his childhood that respect should be earned and trust shouldn't be given to just anybody, he may grow up to be very difficult to befriend and may have trouble trusting even those he cares about and has positive experiences with. Though it is not always the case, often, in unfortunate circumstances, young minds pick up on poor role model behavior, which may follow them around for the rest of their lives or until someone points it out and teaches them to behave differently at least. People may either be receptive to this re-teaching, or they may dismiss it out of hand. This is a character trait that might be attributed to equal parts genetics and upbringing. Let's look at a few examples.

If you enjoy documentaries or true crime, you've probably come across an interview or two where a professional who studies criminal behavior talks about things that happened in childhood that affected how he turned out as an adult. Childhood trauma, such as physical and sexual abuse, parents experiencing a messy divorce or fighting in front of the kids, alcohol or other substance abuse in the home, and many other examples can lead the child to emulate such behavior without a demonstration of other options. If there is nothing done about the influence of these poor role models in the home while a child is growing up, it can be very easy for the child to fall into the same behavior, especially since such experiences are often accompanied by the development of chronic mood disorders like depression, anxiety, difficulty dealing with anger, and personality disorders, the extreme of which have been cited previously, including sociopathic and narcissistic types.

Let us say a young boy named Johnny was sexually abused at the age of 10, and this abuse persisted in the next few years. Childhood and adolescent years are an integral time, not just for physical development, but also for emotional and mental development as well. People who have experienced sexual abuse often grow into adults with a distorted perception of the world and emotional reactions that are tied up with sexual stimulation. Johnny does not develop normally and finds no interest in girls, as all of his sexual stimulation, let's say, is stemming from an abusive male relative. He is too afraid to tell anyone, even his own family, as the perpetrator himself is a trusted member of that family. And this is a tragic reality when it comes to child abuse; children are easier to manipulate and often do not come forward because the perpetrator has played one of a variety of mind games on the child. One of these tactics is to inflict guilt and shame so that the child is too ashamed to come forward and blames himself for the abuse instead. Other children may be controlled by fear, being told that should they tell anyone else about what's going on, this abuser will hurt them more or hurt someone he loves, etc. There are plenty of harmful ways to control children, and this abuse is something that the child will likely carry with him or her for the rest of their lives, even if the abuse is brought to a stop and the perpetrator is brought to justice.

Going back to Johnny, as he develops sexually, his perception and experience with sex alters his patterns of thought and behavior in a way that reflects that experience. He may develop an association between violence and sex and also end up focusing his sexual attention on other young boys. This pattern persists even as he grows older because he has been essentially sexually stilted by this pattern of sexual and emotional abuse he suffered as a boy himself. All of these factors affect one and the other, which results in all sorts of adult deviant behavior and emotional reactions to sexual stimuli, many of which are completely inappropriate.

And, because the individual recognizes that his behavior is deviant, he must devise ways of getting what he wants through not-so-straightforward means, which leads to tactics of dark psychology. Johnny has learned from his own abuser how to condition and control others for sexual gratification, so he is likely more successful than he anticipated when he first puts these lessons into practice himself.

While the development of a personality that favors dark psychology is often cultivated in childhood, this is not always the case. Sometimes, it is learned later in life, when an individual feels he has exhausted all other means, those dark psychology tactics are the only way to achieve a goal. This goal might be money, power, control, fame, esteem, etc. We all tend to have desires along these lines, but most of us develop a corresponding framework of morality and values which would stop us, for example, from setting rumors all around the workplace in an effort to demean another coworker with whom we are in direct competition for a promotion, which brings me to the next area of society where dark psychology often runs rampant—the workplace.

Workplace politics are familiar to a lot of us through sitcoms, movies, social media, and real life. Most of us chuckle in commiseration when a friend tells us about a coworker who is annoying and quirky and who gets on her nerves, etc. We understand that it is very unlikely that we will go through our whole lives without ever having to deal with a difficult coworker or boss. But we make decisions and prioritize the things we care about in order to get past those things or people who are not so enjoyable to be around. And, if a situation at work is just too much to handle, we often make the decision to report behaviors to a boss, or we simply find a new job out of necessity. These actions take place following overt behavior, which is harmful to the company or other coworkers. But how about those things which we don't readily recognize are happening? This is where the clever practitioner of dark psychology tactics takes center stage.

While many strategies utilize the manipulation of people's negative emotions, such as fear and anxiety or shame in our last example with child abuse, sometimes, the strategies alternatively manipulate people's positive emotions in order to build up the practitioner on false pretenses. Skills, such as charisma and public speaking, often go hand-in-hand with these topics because it herds people together in a way that makes it easier to make the desired impression upon multiple people at once. A prime example is in a meeting at work or perhaps in a boardroom, where people might be more inclined to be followers of the outspoken, charismatic participant. These tactics might be used by a member of a team trying to take control or by the leader of the group, or, say, the CEO in a meeting with his underlings. The goal is to win the favor and trust, and respect of those who will prop him up where he wants to be. He can do this through a clever combination of flattery, peer pressure, personality mirroring, and many other strategies which, if done well, will not even be detectable by the people being affected.

These strategies involve paying close attention to the target or targets and basically telling them what they want to hear. It is basic yet complex. Especially when dealing with multiple people and multiple personalities, it becomes important to make each individual feel both unique and important but also to make them feel the pressure to adhere to the group, the rest of which is also in the process of being won over. People don't like to stick out or be different, especially in a work environment where, often, success and prominence depend on things like popularity and how well the person gets along with both coworkers and higher-ups.

As we've discussed, sometimes, dark psychology tactics arise out of necessity when an individual has a goal in conjunction with a limited or very low personal standard regarding ethics, principles, morals, etc. When something you want is more important than how you treat others, dark psychology can be the most effective and efficient way to get things done and achieve personal goals. Let us move into the bigger arena of politics to take a look at how this might—and does—manifest.

Anyone in the business will tell you that the world of politics can be one of the most aggressive, two-faced, and personally challenging work environments on the planet. This is because not every politician has only the good of his people in mind as his goal. We know through research and social experimentation that power and wealth have a strong correlation with corruption. Having these things plays with our psychology in a way that reinforces the idea that power and money and fame mean you are just "better" than anyone else, more capable, more intelligent, etc. This means that what you want and how you want to get there supersedes all other considerations because you believe you know best. Of course, I'm not saying every politician out there is crooked, but politics is definitely a rich ground for pulling out and examining dark psychology tactics in action.

Take the speech, for example. We talked about individuals in the boardroom who may consciously or unconsciously be able to control others' thoughts and opinions through charisma, public speaking skills, and tactics related to flattery and winning over others for personal gain. In political speech, this can happen on a massive scale, as a politician speaks to hundred, thousands, or tens of thousands of people at once. How does he accomplish what he wants to accomplish on this scale?

Obviously, it would be quite challenging to be able to speak a single speech and convince every single listener of the truth and validity of everything you've said, but he can be quite effective if he utilizes some key strategies. One strategy is a careful framing of information that paints your political agenda as much more correct, intelligent, and ethical than that of your opponents. In this strategy of persuasion, the speaker is appealing to the audience's sense of logic and reason. A statement is made; it sounds smart and follows logically. Therefore, the people in the audience begin nodding their heads in agreement. This must be done carefully, and it can't be a bald-faced lie that everyone in the audience knows is untrue. But there is an artful finesse to picking and choosing details involved in the facts and events to frame the event how you want it and how it will put you in a place that has an advantage over the opponent. The audience's emotions aren't really evoked in this strategy, but those who are looking for a candidate whom they feel is smart and capable may be affective greatly through this tactic.

But the politician rarely utilizes one strategy alone in this context. After all, he is trying to reach and persuade as many people as possible within his allotted 60 or 90-minute time slot. And, one of the quickest paths to persuading a complete stranger is through their emotions.

Have you ever seen a speaker open up his speech by telling a story about how he was brought up and how this motivated him to take action and improve the world in a specific way because of his childhood or adolescent experiences? This is a tactic that utilizes the audience's emotions and sensibilities in order to gain their attention and sympathy. The audience is placed in that situation through a brief storytelling episode, then brought emotionally to the conclusion that this individual is an honest man of integrity who is trying to correct something that is wrong in the world, with which he has direct experience. If the story is told in a moving and authentic way, this tactic can be the quickest way to potential voters' hearts.

Our next arena, into which we will go in more detail a little later in this book, is the arena of dating and seduction. Dark psychology strategies run rampant in this area of human society and to a wide array of varying degrees, some of which are quite innocent, while others can be deadly. Let us set the scene.

You are a young woman sitting at a bar alone. You didn't plan on being alone, but your friend is late getting out of work, and you said you would wait for her if she wanted you to. That was about 15 minutes ago.

You're drinking by yourself and absently staring at the TV set above the bar when a man approaches you and asks if he can sit down. He is smiling, well-dressed, and doesn't sound pushy, so you so "okay."

Your conversation is very casual and friendly. He isn't staring creepily at you and isn't using any cheesy pickup lines, so you decide he's nothing to worry about and enjoy your conversation with him. You start volunteering details that he didn't ask for, but you feel comfortable enough to let him know why you're here and that you're waiting for a friend. He starts to share details about his life with you as well. You are impressed that he is willing to show a little vulnerability as he describes how he had a hard day at work and is considering leaving his job for something better. He's dressed pretty nice, you think, so he can't be hurting too bad financially. He compliments how you look and tells you that you seem smart, and he is enjoying his conversation with you. At this point, you start to notice the beginnings of an attraction, and you decide it can't hurt to see where it might go. Your conversation turns a bit flirtatious, and you've had another drink at this time. You are feeling more and more loose and comfortable with this man. You've given him details about your life, but he's also given details about his, so you don't feel like you're being taken advantage of in any way. The thought crosses your mind that you might actually rather spend some more time with this man than hang out with your friend, and you ask if he wants to go somewhere quiet to talk. One thing leads to another from there.

So, what are the nuances to what just happened with this interaction that led to a fun night together with an attractive stranger? There might have been a lot more going on than meets the eye. Granted, there are certainly men out there who are naturally gifted in conversation with women, but a lot of men need to coordinate and plan carefully in order to get where they want to be, especially if they aren't the most attractive man in the room. Luckily for them, women can often be won over with personality and charm rather than looks, as they aren't so superficially inclined as a lot of men. This is where the dark psychology strategies come in.

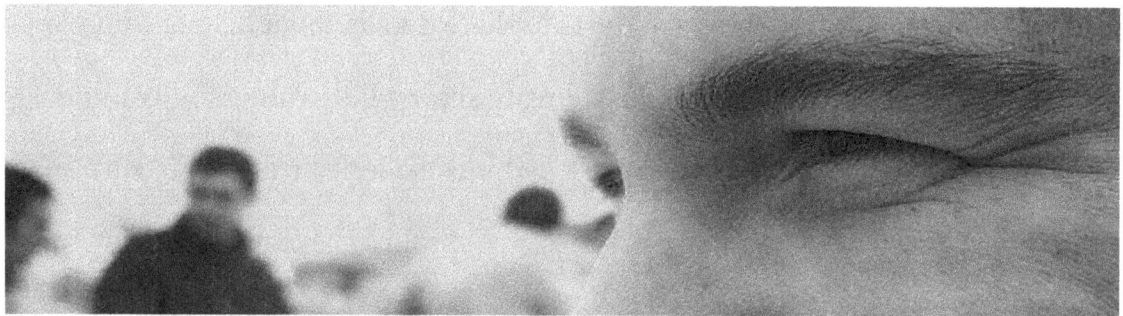

This man approached you in a casual, nonthreatening way. What you didn't realize is that this man has spent a good amount of time just watching you. He did this before approaching you to make educated guesses as to how you were feeling, what your personality might be like as you engaged with other people and the bartender, and whether or not you looked open to engaging in a conversation with a man. He decides that you looked slightly uncomfortable by yourself and guesses that you were probably waiting for someone who was running late to meet you. You probably weren't there specifically to find a date. By approaching casually and at an angle instead of straight toward you, he sent the message that he was just looking for a conversation to pass the time without any kind of agenda. He smiles and gestures in a friendly manner. Releasing personal information made you feel comfortable with letting your guard down a little, as he wasn't really coming on to you. As the conversation progressed, he was careful to share details about his life but also to listen to everything you had to say and engage with you to make you feel important and worth listening to. He listened and remained engaged, sending the message that he was really interested in everything you were talking about. By the end of the night, you decided you were in control of this situation and made the first move, which was exactly as he'd intended in the first place.

These examples we've discussed are just a few of the major areas where dark psychology is always at play in the modern world. Dating and seduction techniques extend to online platforms, as the use of social media makes it possible to groom from a distance and deceive on a whole new level. Young adults and teenagers are especially at risk of this type of predation because of their relative naïve natures and willingness to share information with detecting that someone might be trying to manipulate them.

As we move along, we'll encounter more specific situations and put dark psychology into context as it appears all around us today.

Chapter 3: How Do I Recognize When Dark Psychology Is Being Used?

Learning to recognize when strategies of dark psychology are at work can be a life-saving skill. Often, the situation is not so dire, but decades of research into dark psychology tactics and deviant personality types tell us that many of the most sinister criminals in American history have fallen under the umbrella categorization of types that utilize dark psychology in order to lure victims to their fates. For example, serial killers are often cited as some of the most clever users of dark psychology tactics for the simple reason that, over time, they developed those skills for the sole purpose of scratching that itch they had to kill or abuse victims. Ted Bundy, perhaps one of the most well-known serial killers of all time, got very creative when it came to luring his victims, and a lot of his strategy relied on the "prep" work that took place even before he spoke to the victim.

The first stage of an intelligent practitioner's strategy for using dark psychology is one that remains invisible to the victims, or anyone else, for that matter. This is the observation stage. This is the time the practitioner sets aside to pay very close attention to potential victims in the area, whether he's already chosen his target or is watching the one he wants to zero in on. The target is observed, and the practitioner downloads everything he possibly can about the individual—her movements, the way she speaks to others, her apparent personality type, who she speaks to on a regular basis, where she works, her routines, and others. All of this information is useful for the practitioner trying to discover the most effective way to approach and put into practice whatever strategy he needs to get what he wants. The motivations for using dark psychology on other people are varied and different for each individual who decides to study another human being. This is part of what makes this reality so potentially dangerous. When you don't know the motivations, it is hard to predict behavior.

However, there are several things you can do to better prepare yourself for a dark psychology encounter, and you're already well on your way to fulfilling requirement one, which is educating yourself.

Dark psychology, in large part, depends on the victims not knowing what's going on, hence, "dark" psychology, as we explained in the introductory chapters. People's personalities and vulnerabilities vary from person to person, but, at the same time, there are certain universalities in terms of human behavior that the intelligent dark psychology practitioner exploits to the best of his ability. The whole process is a game, and if you remain one step ahead of your potential adversary, then you can avoid the harm and deceit that will follow an initial approach. Educate yourself and remain skeptical of strangers, especially if you get a bad feeling about the person approaching you.

The next basic practice, next to educating yourself on the basics and strategies of dark psychology, is to simply be aware that not everyone is who they present themselves to be. It is unfortunate that in this modern reality, we cannot really afford to trust our fellow men and women, but there are many people out there just looking and waiting for the opportunity to strike at an unsuspecting victim.

This is not to say that you should never develop new relationships and trust new people, but you should keep your guard up until you've received enough experience and evidence to make you feel comfortable and confident about offering another person your trust.

And it's not like untrustworthy people have never existed in the past. They have, of course, but the landscape of tools at the dark practitioner's disposal had expanded on a massive scale compared to just a few decades ago when there were no Facebook or social media to get an advantage on a target without anyone knowing. Social media, as has been revealed in recent years, can be used as a benevolent social connectivity tool but also for darker intentions that utilize false news stories and emotional manipulation. The 2016 election is a perfect example of what has recently been brought to light as this kind of dark, manipulative techniques in practice. Being aware and vigilant when it comes to allowing strangers to win over your trust and friendship is not different in the digital realm. If anything, you should be even more careful with people online than those you meet on the streets of a busy city.

The internet has provided a means for people all over the world to associate with one another in thousands of different contexts. People use the internet for work, social planning, meeting strangers with similar interests, and dating and meeting potential life partners. All of these require, to some degree, that you relinquish personal information, whether it's a simple email contact or someone whom you want to meet for the first time in person and find a nearby meeting place that is convenient for both of you. Those super popular personality quizzes all over social media provide a huge amount of data and information on people who willingly give this information out. This data doesn't just disappear once you're done with a quiz or whatever form you are filling out.

Data is the most lucrative business and commodity in the world—by a whole lot. And most people are completely unaware of what's going on when they login to their email accounts or go shopping online after clicking an ad on Facebook. Some people simply don't care. They enjoy the fact that they can be catered to and inundated with ads that are targeted to their specific interests. The fact is, there are incredibly detailed profiles of every single human being who is active online, and this information and data are bought and sold all over the place in order to learn how people tick — and then exploit it. Let's go back to the 2016 American presidential election as an example.

The last couple of elections has seen a whole new era emerge in which voters are no longer engaged through in-person campaigning and simple TV ads with a focus on reaching as wide of an audience as possible. With today's connected world and the oceans of data floating around on millions of people all over the country, it has become possible to pinpoint exactly where those voters are. These voters can be persuaded to one political side or the other, "persuadable," and to target them directly through online ads designed to incite fear, anger, empathy, or whatever else seems useful in the endeavor. There is dark psychology going on here, even if there is no face-to-face interaction, and it is very effective.

People who were on the fence in 2016 saw a barrage of misleading or extremely one-sided ads pop up on their Facebook feeds, which sent messages designed to make them see the world the way the advertisers wanted them to. Trump's opponent was painted as an extreme criminalistic individual with ads supporting the tag line "lock her up" and many others. Fake news stories were disseminated in order to convince people of a certain reality and to incite fear and anxiety about whatever the designers wanted them to. People like to think that they are above such psychological ploys and that they are making their own informed decisions, but a lot of us have no idea just how impressionable we all really are, and that is a dangerous reality. Many activists today are trying too hard to eradicate this kind of conduct, especially centering around political elections, and support the idea that personal data should be every person's right and should be protected just like any physical property. This would be one of the greatest challenges a person or organization could ever undertake simply because of the massive presence and ethereal nature of personal data.

So, what can you personally do to protect yourself from certain infringements on your personal data? The answer, to some degree, is nothing. However, you can be proactive in terms of protecting your accounts and taking advantage of all the security measures which are available for people to use online. Banks and credit card companies don't want to put your assets at risk, though people have their credit card numbers stolen all the time. Being vigilant with how you use your cards and personal information online is essential to protect yourself from online fraud. Only use your information on trusted and protected sites. Don't visit sites you don't trust and don't engage in personal conversations with strangers until you have developed a relationship and met them in real life. A person can tell you anything you want to hear from the safety of hiding behind an anonymous screen. Online dating sites have brought people together, and there are lots of wonderful relationships in existence today, which started online, but there are also countless tragedies that have started online, through dating or social media sites. Children and teenagers are especially at risk, as they are often much easier prey than adults who are aware and have experienced the personal dangers involved with interacting with people online. Do not meet someone for the first time in your home or agree to go to their home. Always meet in public until you've developed trust and feel confident you know the person well. Trust your instincts, above all. Don't dismiss a random "bad feeling" if you start to feel this way. Sometimes our subconsciousness knows even more than we think we do about situations and 37 people around us. This is an essential tool when it comes to being approached by a potential dark psychology practitioner as well. The idea of "innocent until proven guilty" does not apply in personal interactions, and you should be on your guard at all times when out in public or when meeting new people.

There is a balance between being able to protect yourself and being open to helping others and forming relationships that develop quickly. While you want to remain aware of all possibilities in public situations and when interacting with people you don't know, you also don't want to cultivate a lifestyle where you are living in fear and seem completely unable to develop trust for people outside of your current circle of family and friends. We, as human beings, are social creatures, and we thrive on developing relationships and being to relate our experiences to those of other people in conversation or other scenarios. Don't be afraid to engage in a conversation with that intriguing man at the bar during a party, but simply be careful about the information you are freely giving out. The group of people actively waiting for an opportunity to manipulate others is much smaller than the group with people who are simply looking to make connections and relate to someone. Don't shut everyone out who crosses your path if you feel like you might be interested in getting to know someone.

A good rule to adhere to in a public situation is never to get drunk with a stranger or group of strangers. This might seem obvious as you sit here and read the statement, but a master manipulator will use whatever he can to make a person feel comfortable enough to drink to the point where they are no longer making good decisions for themselves. If you are at a party or in an atmosphere where there is drinking and partying, always stick close by a friend whom you really know and trust. Don't ever go to a party by yourself where you are obviously alone and vulnerable. Again, it is unlikely, in most situations, that someone is just waiting for someone like that to walk in so he can manipulate you into something you don't want to do, but the chance that there is a manipulator around should be enough to encourage utilizing every safety precaution. When you are accompanied by someone you trust, you are not only protecting yourself, but you are also placing yourself in a position where you can keep an eye on your friend and be her protector as well.

As a side note, I use male pronouns a lot when talking about dark psychology, but women are just as capable and ruthless when it comes to utilizing dark psychology for personal gain. Statistically, there are many more males in the population of violent criminals who fall into the categories of narcissist or sociopath. But it is not unheard of for a female to be the aggressor in an insidious dark psychology situation, perhaps with a significant other or family member. The fact that we hear more about male perpetrators and manipulators than women does not mean that those females do not exist in the population. There is simply a different set of tools at the woman's disposal, and they are used a little bit differently.

In addition to learning all you can about dark psychology strategy, it is also very helpful to understand, as much as possible, about human nature and how people can become vulnerable in social situations. We've touched on several at work according to different purposes.

In the common scenario of a man trying to pick up a woman in a public setting, flattery and charm are often used in order to get the woman to lower her guard and feel good about the budding relationship. Knowing ahead of time that things like flattery have a very real effect on emotions and decision-making will help give you a bit of an advantage if this situation unfolds for you. The same is true in the reverse situation. Women can use flattery and charm and make a complete stranger feel like a superhero in a very short amount of time. This is because we are all susceptible to the positive feelings that arise when someone is complimenting us. We simply can't help it, and you shouldn't feel like a weak-minded person when this happens. The key is to recognize what's going on and not fall into a trap where you are releasing additional information to this person simply because he or she makes you feel good. It could be sincere, as we have mentioned, but it might be an act.

If you are with a friend and someone is approaching him or her, and you get a bad feeling about the interaction, don't be afraid to interrupt on your friend's behalf. Some people may be hesitant in this scenario and feel that it isn't his or her place to get in between what might look like a really pleasant interaction. But, if this person is really your friend, take it upon yourself to protect him or her from potential predatory threats, especially if there is alcohol involved. You can do this by staying nearby and not actually interrupting in an explicit sense. If you can, keep an eye on the interaction and observe how your friend is behaving and interacting. Is she drinking more than she should? Does it look like this person is showing her compliments and flattery? These are such common tactics; it is worth looking into if you suspect that the person's intentions are not completely benign.

The last topic to discuss in terms of recognizing dark psychology in action is a much more difficult one to deal with and, often, is not recognized until things have escalated to a point where someone is really getting hurt, emotionally or physically. I'm talking about dark psychology in practice that involves a close friend, family member, or colleague. It is a much simpler issue to discuss how you can protect yourself from complete strangers, but what can you do when it is your own family member or partner? This can be an incredibly painful and complex problem to solve, but the most common impairment in this situation on the part of the victim is the factor of denial.

We simply don't want to believe that someone we have loved and trusted for a long time is capable of harmful and manipulative techniques. The abusive husband, the son who is a drug addict, the domineering mother or father — all of these situations can be crippling for life for the victim if the behavior is never recognized or addressed.

Perhaps the first thing to wrap your mind around in this situation is that no one is perfect, no one is an angel, and we all have hang-ups. If someone you love and trust tries to gaslight you and put you in a state of confusion, you have to recognize that this is really happening and that, in many cases, you simply can't "fix" other people when they make the decision to use these dark psychology strategies. Narcissists don't magically rid themselves of narcissism when someone speaks reason to them. Neither does the sociopath, in most cases. Someone who is manipulative has chosen this lifestyle because he or she has been able to get what he or she wants in the past using these tools. It's as simple as that. It may be incredibly painful to realize, but it is imperative that an individual removes herself from the situation as soon as possible when she recognizes that things don't seem quite right and there are inconsistencies in her partner's or friend's behaviors. Red flags have to

be paid attention to—it could save your life or the life of someone you know and love.

In the following chapters, we will get into deeper detail about specific manipulative techniques and several different examples of motivations that can lead someone to engage in these techniques as the most efficient way to achieve a goal or get what a person wants from others.

Chapter 4: Manipulation Techniques

Manipulation itself comes in many forms, along with varying intentions and motivations. Some of them are used with malicious intent, while other people simply use the principles of persuasion in order to make a sale or convince someone of their point of view. Dark psychology is often brought into discussion when we are talking about the absolute worst example of manipulation tactics, though technically, magicians using sleight of hand to impress a group of children is a dark psychology technique.

I make this point as we move on to discuss specific techniques so that you have a broader idea of what we are discussing when we say dark psychology and manipulation. It is likely that you did not pick up this book to learn about magicians' technique, so you will notice that most of the dark psychology techniques we discuss in this book are used most often for decidedly malicious or selfish reasons on the part of the dark psychology practitioner. Let us begin with persuasion.

Persuasion

Aristotle outlined three modes of persuasion under the terms logos, pathos, and ethos. Each of these persuasion modes is a good illustration of the different ways people try to "get in" with other people with the specific intention of getting them to believe the same way you do about a certain belief system or to get something from them willingly that they had not been inclined to give before the conversation began. As we discussed earlier, there are many different paths available to take in order to fulfill this goal. You can appeal to a person's sense of logic, you can appeal strictly to emotions, or you can appeal to others by giving the impression that you are someone others should follow based on things like strong character, charisma, morals, and ethics, etc. Logos is the term related to appealing to logic, ethos is related to appealing to emotions, and pathos is the strategy of presenting yourself as a strong and worthy leader for others to follow. Each of these is effective in different ways, and oftentimes they are used in conjunction in order to reach lots of different people and personalities at the same time. We can see all of these strategies in action by looking at the example of a political speech.

In a speech where there are many gathered to listen, it is quite impossible to pinpoint one singular strategy that is likely to touch everyone listening in the exact same way. For this reason, most speechwriters are going to aim to cover a lot of ground in terms of persuasive techniques so that they gain as much attention and affinity toward the candidate as possible.

When it comes to stirring people's emotions, many speakers will move toward storytelling as a way to demonstrate where the person's heart is and where their motivations are coming from for running for office and the things they hope to accomplish while in office. If the speaker can make an emotional connection, and listeners believe that he is sincere, then they will gradually start to view the speaker as pure of the heart where that particular issue is concerned. They experienced something that made them take action to improve the situation for anyone else who might have to go through what he went through, etc. Motivation like this comes off as pure and honest, and kind-hearted, and this can often be enough to move a voter who is on the fence towards this particular candidate's side in an election.

Logos is an approach that focuses on appealing to the collective audience's logic and reason. The speaker will present his views in a way that makes sense or what appears to make sense. Arguments and framing facts is an art in itself, which often entails picking out details and facts here and there, which serve to prop up the speaker's views and opinions and omits anything that might plant a seed of doubt in the listeners' minds. This is something that politicians and talking heads often call "spin." Politicians and their writers often spin the facts to make their own positions look like the logical, correct side to be on. Logical arguments must follow a line of reasoning that makes sense to the listener. Otherwise, there is no impact. The speaker doesn't want to make anyone listening to him feel too dumb to understand, but he also wants to make himself look like he really knows what he's talking about. The use of facts and figures, statistics, and citing what most people recognize as a reputable source of information are all things that will help prop the logical argument.

Finally, in a pathos line of argument, the focus is on how the speaker himself is being presented. What is the first impression you want to make on those people in the audience who are looking at you, watching your mannerisms, and hearing you speak? When the pathos mode is active, there is usually a great deal of attention given to how the speaker looks, down to the last detail. What clothes is the speaker wearing? What does this say about him or her? What details might suggest positive things to those watching? Believe it or not, there is a great deal of evidence in research to suggest that people are often swayed to voting for someone based on how much better they look physically than their competitors.

And this often becomes a factor even when it is not obvious or apparent to the person making the judgment. People are drawn to those who look healthy and fertile, and this often means the younger candidates with handsome features and better skin have an automatic leg up on the competition if they are deemed not as good-looking.

But aside from how the speaker looks, a lot of attention is given to how the speaker will interact with the audience, not just concerning the specific words coming out of his mouth but how he will move and use body language to convey an impression he wants from the listeners. A lot of this body language is recorded and has an influence on a subconscious level, which we will discuss in more detail in a later chapter. How often will the speaker use his hands, make eye contact, or use gestures to elucidate what he is saying?

The words in his speech themselves will be focused on forming a reflection of good character and whatever else the politician wishes to convey to his audience. The words must be chosen carefully to avoid sounding like boasting without enough foundation or evidence. The ideal impression would be that a listener finds the speaker charismatic, sincere, and honest about his goals for the future and for his political party. If the candidate is a veteran, this will likely be a highlight of the speech as an introduction according to the pathos mode of persuasion. The audience already has a great deal of information and data, which automatically connotes with the word "veteran," and so a lot of the work will be done for the speaker just by mentioning the specifics of when and where he served. Other categorizations work in a similar way, such as working for nonprofit and charity organizations connoting generosity and kind-hearted, selfless nature.

Pathos, logos, and ethos can all work on much smaller scales and in a one-on-one situation. The salesman who has a couple of minutes of interaction on the sales floor with potential customers will employ tactics that engage the person's emotions through need. He will often pitch the customer in the form of a well-reasoned argument for why the product will bring some benefit to the customer's life, and he will also portray himself as someone whom the customer can trust and respect based on a professional, congenial, and friendly demeanor and mannerisms.

Taking Over a Room/Becoming "Alpha"

This area of manipulation happens on a group scale that is not necessarily as large as a political speech. When we talk about the alpha of a group, we're talking about the unspoken (or spoken) dominant individual in a group, male, who is the leader, most popular, etc. The term is used to describe a person with many dominant personality traits. Here, we'll talk about the process of winning over a group of people who had been strangers and are now aware and interested in this individual. These tactics are often used in a situation when a practitioner wants to gain the attention of someone in the room. Perhaps there is someone important present who could help the individual move forward at work or in some other endeavor. Or perhaps there is a woman he wants to get the attention of, but she is always surrounded by people and tends to favor the popular, powerful type. For any of these reasons, the following plan of action is often cited as a strategy that can work like magic within as little as a few hours.

As with pretty much every successful practitioner of dark psychology tactics, this individual—let's call him John—has put in some prep work. He has gathered as much information as he possibly could through observation, perhaps a little online digging to check out social media profiles, etc. He gets familiar with the type and function of the gathering itself. Is it primarily social? What kind of people are the most important ones there? Who is hosting? Who are the influential figures that will be present? Before the event, John must have a singular, focused goal for his actions. Let's say he is trying to win over the CEO at his company because there is a potential position opening up that would come with a substantial pay raise, and John really wants to be considered. There is a lot of competition in the form of very talented and skilled employees as well as people who have been with the company for a very long time. John has worked at the company long enough to know that the people in power like motivation, drive, charisma, and the ability to talk smoothly and with confidence, especially when it comes to meetings with potential clients.

John's first action of preparation is to be sure to dress the part. He pays attention to cleanliness, his teeth are sparkling white, and his clothes are freshly cleaned and ironed. He might choose to invest in a brand that is similar to the type of clothing he's seen his higher-ups wear on the occasions he's interacted with them. Mirroring will come into play a little later, and subtle things like wearing similar clothing will play into this specific tactic nicely.

The next important consideration is to make sure he arrives promptly at the start of the event. He doesn't want to show up too early, which could be annoying and inconvenient, and he doesn't want to show up too late, which might signal disinterest and turn off those people who have already had better impressions from the other competition. Now it's time to mingle.

The goal for the next hour or so is for John to go around and introduce himself to as many people as he possibly can. He doesn't just go shake hands with them and move on.

Rather, he introduces himself to one, and then the rest of the circle then listens to what the conversation topic is at the moment of his arrival. He will stand with confidence, shoulders back, head up, and listen to what's going on. Careful not to interrupt or appear rude, he waits for an opportune time to interject with something very thoughtful, intelligent, or witty. If he doesn't really know much about what's being talked about, he might fall back on being entertaining through a well-timed joke, or he might give compliments to the speakers and express interest in the topic which he could learn more about or, even better, all of these things within the same conversation. In these few minutes, he has now managed to make himself known to this group, expressed an interested and entertaining personality, and ingratiated himself to the speakers by complimenting their intelligence. All of these things are moving him forward, even if he hasn't directly addressed his main target yet.

As human beings, we are very social animals, and we take a lot of cues about how to feel about other people by the way others react and interact with that individual. How often have you been in the middle of a crowd where one person starts talking loudly about someone nearby who smells bad or is dressed weird, and people all around within earshot start looking around and automatically making grimacing facial expressions as if they are the ones who have directly interacted with this weird, smelly individual. We are more susceptible to social influence than a lot of us like to think, and this overconfidence is something someone like John will be taking advantage of over time.

Once John feels he has met his goals with this first group, he moves on to the next. It is important for John's success that he does not go from group to group, repeating the exact same comments and behaviors as the group before. There may be a lot these people have in common, but they are all individuals, too, with unique personalities, insights, and behaviors. The next group may be talking about a completely different topic about which John has some knowledge. Again, without interrupting or completely hijacking the conversation, he waits for a good moment to slowly involve himself in the conversation. But he is careful not to spout facts and figures to impress people with his knowledge. One of the main things at the front of John's mind is that at the end of the day, people just want to be entertained. If he can be entertaining, he is going to be remembered. No one really remembers the boring guy who could recite a bunch of boring information like he's reading from a book. While it might be impressive, that probably isn't what most of the attendants are looking to spend their time doing. As John speaks, he is also careful to listen and ask people questions as he goes along. He knows that people really respond well to a few specific things when it comes to casual conversation—talking about themselves and hearing their own names. John will involve both tactics in his conversation rounds as he works his way around the room.

What starts to happen during this process is that John is making positive impressions all around the room with many different guests. As he moves, he might even be starting to get people to follow him around the room with interest in what he has to say further. He may stop at the refreshments table to interact with whoever is standing there, taking the opportunity to say something funny as he takes the measure of the different personalities. Again, he is careful not to just repeat his behavior and comments with everyone in the room. He may come up against someone who does not look like she is having fun and instead approaches with a little less of the pep he has carried with him thus far. He might express that he's noticed she doesn't look like she's having fun and ask if there is something bothering her and if she would like to talk about it. Another tactic would be to say something funny and see if he can get a positive reaction out of her. This would be a big win, as anyone who has ever been in a bad mood often appreciates someone who can chase away the clouds, even if it's just for a few minutes.

And finally, the moment arrives when he has the opportunity to meet and interact with his main target. If all has gone well up to this point, John may be brought over by someone who has taken a liking to John and offers to introduce them. This will likely resonate with John's target. Let's call him Mr. Carter. Mr. Carter sees the enthusiasm being exuded from John's acquaintance, and this sends a positive signal to Mr. Carter's subconscious that this John fellow might be alright, even if he isn't directly aware of it.

John is introduced, and now, he must up his game and become hyper-focused. Again, the skill of observation is going to be very important here. John must show interest in his target's words and actions, as well as offer an entertaining yet knowledgeable and charismatic interaction. One of the key strategies he may use here, and which is used widely in similar situations, is the tactic of mirroring.

Mirroring is all about assimilating subtle mannerisms, behavior patterns, and aspects of someone's personality into your own behavior and speech patterns as you are speaking with the target. The reason this works to help you ingratiate yourself quickly to a target is that human beings on a fundamental, evolutionary level respond more positively to things and people that appear and feel familiar. It is a signal of safety and of like-mindedness that will bypass any negative impressions, assuming it is done in a way that does not look like mocking. This would be a disaster, as no one likes to be mocked, and it would be a major insult, to destroy all the gain John has made at the party so far.

For this reason, effective mirroring is very subtle. John doesn't want to look like he's mocking Mr. Carter, but he wants to move into a position where he will recognize and appreciate certain important commonalities. Some of the safe ways to do this include sharing similar political views, opinions on business practice, past experiences, and personality traits. The personality traits, which will be the most forthcoming upon first interacting with Mr. Carter, will reflect how outgoing, personable, and open he is. If Mr. Carter is having a good time and uses lots of big gestures, like opening his hands and using his hands to gesture while he is talking, then John needs to get on his level and appear outgoing, motivated, and like he is having a good time. He will also make his points with enthusiasm, using lots of gestures to mirror Mr. Carter's passion for his own views.

On the other hand, if Mr. Carter is quite reserved and conservative in his conversation style, John will mirror this environment and keep his conversation and interactions reserved, though he might take a risk and tell a joke in order to be entertaining once he feels he's established some level of rapport with his target.

At the end of the interaction, John should have a pretty good idea of how he is doing based on Mr. Carter's progression throughout the conversation. Has he continued on and progressively become more open in his topics? Has he released information that he might not have if he didn't feel comfortable with John? These and many more are questions that will go through John's mind as the conversation comes to an end. He will also pay close attention to how Mr. Carter chooses to end the conversation. An open invitation or movement toward a second meeting is a great signal, and this will tell John that the interaction has been successful.

There are many other possibilities for dark psychology tactics that may have been present in just this one night's event, and we will continue to touch on others and progress through how these might play out in different scenarios. On a conversational level, there are less covert but no less effective tactics that people practice on a daily basis, even if they aren't overtly trying to win someone over for a specific goal that they are aware of.

Flattery is one of the most common things people use to get on people's good sides, whether they are trying to pick up a date or form new friendships and alliances. People enjoy flattery when it doesn't feel like the person is trying too hard and being insincere. Think of a time when you were in line at a store or other public place, and a complete stranger takes the time to stop and compliment you on something. Maybe you look nice in your outfit, or they like your hairstyle, etc. This feels good because someone had gone out of their way to address a stranger when there really wasn't anything to gain from the measure. It can turn your whole day around when someone compliments you like this. It feels just as good to receive compliments at work from coworkers or when you are out with your friends. When it is done right, flattery can instantly ingratiate someone who had simply been a complete stranger before and move them quickly into the realm of acquaintance. However, flattery can also go sideways when the target picks up on the fact that you were only flattering them as a precursor to asking for something. We see this played out in sitcoms all the time when a character approaches the boss and offers a silly compliment before asking for something that he is pretty sure the boss will say no to. If he can "butter him up" first, he knows there is some slight possibility he will improve his chances of getting what he wants. This can really put a person off if this tactic is revealed and the behavior is too obvious, and he may completely shut down the conversation as he realizes he is being duped.

Online Grooming

The last area of dark psychology tactics we'll discuss in this chapter pertains to online behaviors and interactions. Relative to other dark psychology realms and tactics, this arena is new and still being researched and explored, especially in relation to how people interact and form relationships online.

Grooming refers to a practice where a person talks to a target, usually young and naïve, in the most successful instances, and develops a relationship with them online. Tragic accounts relay the succession of events in detail, as will the following.

A young girl named Amanda is very active online with social media accounts, and she constantly posts things on Facebook, Instagram, Twitter, and other sites, which give her followers a pretty good idea of how she spends her time from day to day and who she likes to interact with. She enjoys taking selfies and making herself look as cool and pretty as possible. She also uses filters and such which make her look more attractive, and she likes how sometimes she can make herself look older and more mature from the right angle.

An online predator will often look for signs like this as a way to pinpoint prospective victims, but it also has a lot to do with the wrong place at the wrong time. A predator attracted to an individual decides to move on his plan to groom her through flattery and constant attention. When this is shut down right away, often, the predator will simply move on. But if the grooming is successful, the predator will receive positive signals that his ploy is working when the attention he is offering is acknowledged almost all the time, and there are positive responses. The online groomer will continue these interactions and slowly introduce suggestions that move the relationship further. At first, just innocently flirting and constantly bantering are the main interactions going on. But then, he will throw out a more sexually-oriented comment to see if the young teenager takes the bait. If she does, then he's got a green light to keep going, as this child seems to be fooled. If the child is put off by the comment by not responding to the predator, he might hold back and slow things down until he can reform that sense of trust and comfort that was presented before. Some predators spend a great deal of time online talking to young women under the pretense of being someone they are not. They follow those leads which seem promising and abandon those that don't seem to be going anywhere.

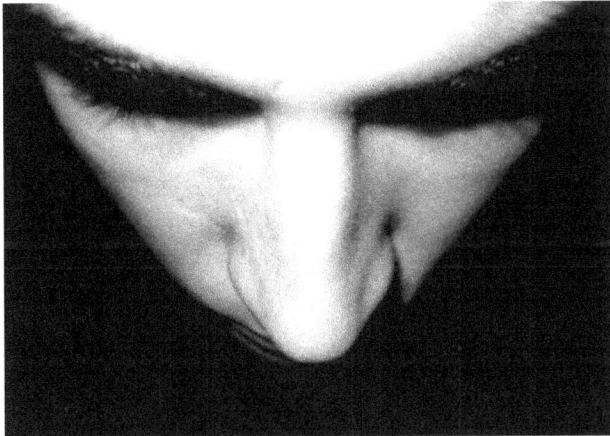

The ultimate goal in a lot of these grooming instances is to get the child to agree to meet in person somewhere that is private, like the predator's home. Agreeing to something like this suggests a very strong degree of trust and naivete about the possibility that someone is pursuing something he shouldn't. In her mind, she is meeting with a cute, playful young guy who is attractive. Perhaps this will be her first boyfriend, and she blinded by the excitement of it all. Some of these cases end in very tragic ways, and this reinforces the importance of getting the message through to young people that they can't trust everyone they meet online and that they should be very wary of this grooming tactic so that they recognize it if it happens to them. Many kids have interacted online with a predator who has moved on, and they never have any idea that this was what took place.

Chapter 5: What Is Mind Control?

When most people hear the phrase "mind control," they associate things they might have heard in the movies or on a TV show. It sounds like a science-fiction concept, and there are plenty of people who do not believe that it is possible to control another person's mind. And to some degree, they are correct. But the term mind control does not mean the same thing to everyone, and when psychologists use the term, they are not talking about turning another human being into a robot for personal use. The arts surrounding mind control are much more subtle and more powerful than most people are familiar with.

Mind control reached public consciousness through media like science fiction movies, but there are practices which can have a direct influence on a subject's psychological state. Even the manipulation techniques through social media ads is a form of mind control in which there is a subtle influence going on that the target is completely unaware of. The idea of mind control practices is not to turn a human being into an automaton but to influence decision-making on a level where the individual believes they are making the decision or reacting under their own volition. Let's look at a few different examples of mind control.

Hypnosis

Hypnosis is another term that comes with a lot of connotation straight from science fiction movies. When people are hypnotized in movies or TV shows, they are often completely catatonic and under complete control of the hypnotist. This is certainly untrue, but there is a great misunderstanding in the greater culture about the nature and intention of hypnosis.

Hypnosis is often used in the context of treatment for people who are suffering from memory impairment as a symptom of a bigger problem. It can also be used as a form of therapy in order to work through traumatic experiences and encourage the movement of emotional processing, like grief.

The hypnosis therapist is not someone with special power over people's brains. Their practice rather stems from full engagement and openness to empathy directed toward a patient for different means. The essential ingredient to a successful hypnosis therapy is an established trust and respect between therapist and patient. The patient goes into the process with an understanding that her part in the process is not just to sit back and let things happen. The patient has a responsibility to open up to the process and allow herself to become vulnerable and impressionable. She goes willingly and follows the therapist, where he leads. So, in this way, there is a partnership going on with in the process instead of this popular notion that the therapist can simply put people under a "spell." In fact, there are plenty of people who are simply less impressionable and open to the process of hypnosis, and therefore, would see no benefit from an attempt.

In a hypnotic session which aims to reach back and pull memories from a patient's mind, which has put up a barrier to protect it from painful experiences, the hypnosis therapist gently guides the patient, over time, close to the origin of those memories that are trying to be retrieved. The patient must let go and be willing to follow the instructions and suggestions, almost like someone leading her by the hand as she walks through memory lane. In this way, the patient may be able to stumble upon memories of repressed experiences that are working to hold her back or hurt her emotionally, seemingly without her control. Once these repressed memories can be addressed, the patient can work past the pain through therapy and refresh her mind to come to a place where she is fully functional and able to process and develop new memories and emotions.

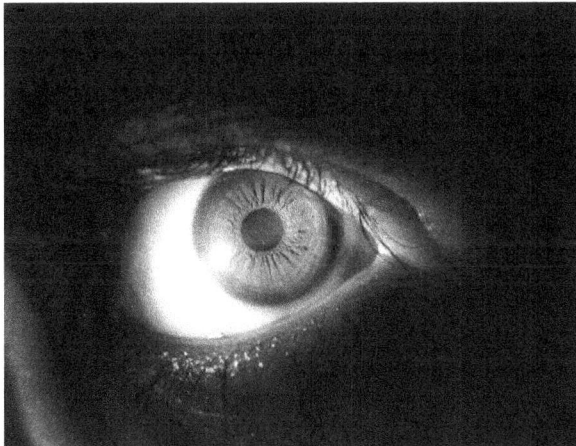

Hypnosis is also used to treat patients who suffer from PTSD through engaging with and working through repressed experiences or experiences which haunt the patient day and night. Each process is different, as well as individual outcomes. Hypnosis has become quite stigmatized, and many people look at the process with a skeptical view, but there are others who praise the process of hypnosis, claiming the process is responsible for great recoveries through consistent practice.

Gaslighting

Next, let's take a look at a much more insidious form of mind control—that of gaslighting. If you've never heard the term gaslighting, then count yourself fortunate for never having had to experience it. Or, perhaps you just didn't recognize or know there was a term for this particular manipulative technique.

Gaslighting refers to a process where the abuser convinces the victim over time that what he or she believed was real is questionable. Often, this happens through a long series of denials, in which the victim tries to get an abuser to acknowledge wrongdoing while the abuser consistently denies that any abuse is going on. At first, the victim may be enraged and become insistent, throwing the clear evidence or the facts she knows to be true in the abuser's face, but the abuser remains steadfast in his denials. Over time, this confrontational attitude deteriorates, and the victim is broken down. After a while, the once confident and confrontational victim starts to succumb to doubts and confusion as to what he or she is actually experiencing. The effects of this kind of abuse are long-lasting and often intense, especially if the abuse is happening during childhood or adolescent years.

When a parent or guardian engages in gaslighting, the child becomes incredibly confused and ashamed that he or she cannot grasp what is going on. This damage can extend to the child's personality as well as his or her emotional intelligence and development. This kind of abuse is not something that a person gets over quickly with a few sessions of therapy. It is also one of the most dangerous forms of long-term manipulation because of the mental damage that can be inflicted.

Gaslighting can also be just one ingredient in a potent cocktail of manipulation techniques, which work together with other tactics in order to enforce control and manipulate a partner in a romantic relationship. Once a bond of love and trust is formed, partners who suddenly switch gears and become abusive can be incredibly hurtful and wield power to inflict a large amount of pain and suffering on the partner or those who love the abuser. We hear in the news sometimes about an abusive husband or a domestic situation where the victim in the partnership simply refuses to let go or get out of the situation. Sometimes we may be tempted to judge these individuals as if to say, "why doesn't she just leave?" The truth is, there is often a whole lot more going on than meets the eye.

If the situation were simple, then perhaps we can imagine an abuser coming straight out one day out of the blue and beginning to abuse his wife. The wife sees the behavior, knows she is in danger, and then leaves immediately to stay with a friend or other family member. But domestic abuse situations are rarely so simple. There are mind games that are likely being played on the part of the abuser, and these games can work their way deep into a victim's mind so that the victim may believe preposterous things about the situation or remain in complete denial that there is anything serious happening. Let's look at an example scenario to see how this might play out to get a better understanding of these mind games.

Mandy is a newlywed and has just married her high school sweetheart, Danny. They are young and in love and reflect that kind of puppy love that makes it seem like the two of them just can't get enough of each other. They are both looking for jobs and for an apartment to move into. During high school, there was a structure that supported them, and their parents have been helping out to the best of their abilities. They don't have children yet, and they are planning to become financially stable before planning for a family.

Abuse and domestic turmoil often follow an event or series of events in which the structure and support that the couple had been used to have been destroyed or changed in some way, and they could not seem to go back. This could happen in the form of a job opportunity falling through, an unexpected child getting in the way, parents who stop supporting the kids financially, or suffering from death in the family. All these are example situations that might upend all the couple's plans for the near future. When something drastic happens to change a person's way of life at a time when they don't have someone to lean on or some kind of support network, the consequences can be severe and long-lasting. In this case, we have a young couple who is in love but have yet to face any real-life challenges that marriage and life after school often entail. Abuse may begin to rear its head after the initial period known as the "honeymoon" phase, which is the time when everything feels perfect because you are consumed by love for the other person.

Their underlying personality traits have not shown up yet because both partners are still trying to put their best feet forward and present the best of what they are in order to be as attractive as possible.

But marriage isn't about only seeing the best parts of people. And sometimes, there are things about a spouse that are much darker or completely unexpected. It is during this time that the couple goes through a real-time of growing pains, in which they must decide what they really want out of a partner and whether or not they can accept the person's perceived flaws through the strength of their bond.

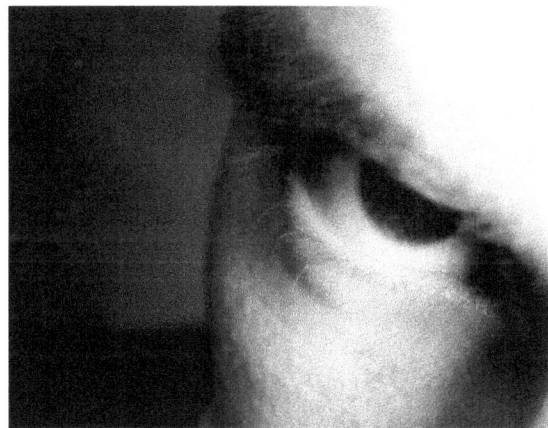

In Mandy and Danny's case, Danny starts off by just becoming distant as the months pass by as he is looking for stable work. They are no longer in school, and Mandy is looking at college opportunities in the area. Perhaps Danny is really struggling much more than Mandy, but he feels like he can't tell her about it because it makes him feel weak. Instead, he lets his anxiety and emotions fester until he is driven to take them out on someone.

Danny becomes verbally abusive, and Mandy fights back, contributing to some of the worst fights they've ever had in their short relationship. At this point, personality traits are coming to light that perhaps neither of them have seen before in themselves. As Mandy begins to push away, Danny sees that he is on his way to losing his wife if he can't convince her to stay. He may go into a panic mode and begin reaching toward manipulation as a response to this anxiety, or he may decide that control is the only way to calm himself down. The impetus for turning to manipulative and controlling techniques in a relationship can be one of a myriad of different things, but often, the action comes from fear of losing the partner, rooted in jealousy, or a fear of being alone.

In the beginning, Danny may even be successful in convincing himself that he is not manipulative, but anyone on the outside might see differently, having seen what is happening. Danny begins to beg forgiveness after he has hurt his young wife, and the two of them engage in long conversations after their fights in an effort to reconcile; and Danny assures Mandy that he won't behave that way again and everything will be alright. He showers her with love in these moments, and she believes his words because of a combination of wanting to believe him and the effort he's put into coming off as completely sincere. In the back of his mind, he may truly think that he is getting past these behaviors, but if the anxiety and underlying mood disorder are not addressed, then there is nothing to stop this pattern of emotional reaction in the face of acute stress.

The next time they fight, he abuses her verbally and calls her harsh names that he has never used before. The anger feels more intense and uncontrollable, but again, after a while, they end up talking and getting through the night, agreeing that they still love each other. The last time this happened, emotional manipulation through flattery and expressions of love worked to calm his wife down, so he

68

engages in these practices again, even if he doesn't feel them to be completely true . He is prideful and doesn't want to acknowledge any possibility that his anger and frustrations may be getting out of control. In an effort to distract himself, he pulls away from his wife and sees that when he does this, she becomes desperate and willing to do anything to get him to come back and open up to her. He sees that he can use this to his advantage as a means of control and gradually engages in a pattern of pulling away and coming back to shower her with apologies and love. This cycle is enough to sustain her but also painful enough that she becomes desperate to win him back each time he pulls away. He never fully leaves her in these dark times. Perhaps he just goes to a friend's house for a few nights. And he sends her text messages to string her along, assuring her that he is working to become a better husband and doesn't want to hurt her. She believes these things based on the faith that she has in the good sides of him that she has seen, heard, and felt, though these aspects seem to have faded.

We can see in this scenario that this pattern of behavior evolves and seems to form out of negative emotional experiences. Emotional pain is some of the hardest pain that humans have to deal with, and sometimes, people go to desperate measures to avoid it, even if it means hurting the ones we love in order to ensure that we don't lose them. This, of course, is not love. It is possessiveness and fear, and hopefully, Mandy realizes the type of toxic cycles that have formed out of her relationship and begins to seek help to get out of it.

Cults

The cult is an interesting topic because there are often lots of different manipulative and dark psychology techniques going on at the same time. Once a person has been hooked through some kind of promise of emotional or spiritual fulfillment, the human mind often works against itself in the way illustrated above when the object of desire is something we want so badly that we ignore red flags going up in our minds about the situations we've gotten ourselves into. When we are desperate to believe in something or someone, there are no limits to how deep we can bury our heads into the sand in order to give ourselves the illusion that we are living the way that we want and getting what we want out of this lifestyle. This has been the case for many people who have come forward years after having been sucked into a cult that was found to be practicing very unsavory things behind the curtain, including child abuse and other forms of sexual abuse, verbal abuse, torture, etc. Even those who may have seen these behaviors going on were sometimes too buried in the mire of the cult's beliefs and under so much influence that they were able to turn a blind eye and convince themselves that there was nothing really immoral going on.

This should ring a bell in relation to the psychological experiments we talked about earlier in which people were able to convince themselves that the higher-ups and people in control knew better, and what they were doing was completely sanctioned by "smarter" people with nothing but good intentions. The Milgram experiment illuminated this aspect of human psychology quite clearly and in a fascinating way. It often held up a light to understand a little bit better how a malicious movement like the fascist party could have risen to power under such seemingly immoral conduct and motivations. The human mind is a powerful and complex mechanism, and the power of social influence should never be underestimated.

Chapter 6: Dark Psychology and Seduction

Dark Psychology in the realm of seduction is our next topic, and one which has caused a large amount of heartbreak, trauma, and tragedy for countless men and women. But the application of dark psychology when it comes to seduction and the romantic world is, again, part of a spectrum of tactics, not all of which are overtly malicious.

Someone who enters the dating world and presents only the best sides of himself is practicing a form of dark psychology in that he is presenting a sort of "white lie" as he hides the things about himself that he thinks a woman may not like or may prompt negative judge about him without first getting to know him. We are all guilty of making false, negative assumptions about people sometimes before we even talk to them, so a degree of this is totally understandable. But when the lie persists, and there is never a fully open two-way exchange of trust and respect, then there is fertile ground for turmoil and even abuse.

In this chapter, we will be discussing the more malicious applications of dark psychology within the realm of seduction.

One of the most dangerous things about the practice of dark psychology in romantic relationships is that not only can the effects be devastating and have long-lasting effects, but the perpetrator also often carries out these insidious strategies over a long time while distorting and playing with the target's emotions. When a person has successfully gained the trust of another individual, that person becomes very vulnerable in the realm of emotions because trusting someone means believing in positive motivations and good decision-making even when you don't have all the facts or do not have a front-row seat to what's going on.

For example, if a married woman finds out her husband is going on a trip for work, she may or may not feel uneasy about the situation. If the relationship has a healthy amount of trust and respect without any prior infractions, then it is likely the woman will not feel too much anxiety about the prospect of her husband going away for a few days, much less the idea that he is going to cheat on her with a coworker. If the husband has that intention, then having established trust beforehand ensures that he is likely to get away with his intentions without worrying about his wife having the slightest suspicions. But, chances are, a man who just wants to sleep around is not going to go through the trouble of establishing a stable marriage for years before enacting his plans. And it would be difficult for this man to convince his wife of a completely different persona for that period of time, and the effort would not be worth it unless there were additional hidden goals motivating those efforts. A man who goes through this much work to establish a different persona from his own for the sake of self-betterment and advantage ventures into the realm of the dark triad persona set, which we will get deeper into in the next chapter.

For the purposes of this chapter, we will focus on the seduction that takes place at the very beginning of a relationship. As mentioned previously, the use of dark psychology may not be a focused, conscious effort, but simply some advice a person got from a friend or something he read online on a dating forum. For whatever reason, the dark psychology practitioner in this scenario will begin with some careful observation and information gathering before making his first move. Just as in the prior example of an individual trying to take over a room and become an alpha-like presence in the room, someone with a singular target whom he wishes to win over within as little as a few minutes will begin by making sure he's chosen the best target for his intentions. It's not enough to just pick out someone whom he finds attractive. He must also look out for additional signs that this woman is going to be open to an approach at all, let alone a friendly conversation. The setting itself could be just about anywhere that it would be appropriate to approach someone you don't know and introduce yourself. The environment may be a place like a party or a bar or some other public place where people hang out regularly. But we could also be talking about a quiet coffee shop, a park, or outside a bus stop. People meet acquaintances in all kinds of places, and, once the target is chosen, the place where the practitioner will want to make his first move must be a place where it is going to be comfortable and convenient to carry out a conversation. For example, he wouldn't want to meet his target while she's busy on her way to work or obviously trying to accomplish a task that demands her full attention. Rather, he wants to catch her somewhere where she is relaxed and just enjoying something without a lot of stress involved. People in this environment and state of mind will be more open to unplanned meetings and events, and he will want his target to be as comfortable and open as possible.

One of the most important decisions that the practitioner will make when using dark psychology in seduction is choosing the target. We often watch programs or news reports of someone being abducted or fooled into doing something a person didn't want to do, and you might think, "I would never do that." Well, the truth is, most of us can be overconfident when it comes to making judgments and reading another person's character. Sometimes, we are correct, and other times, there is a very clever dark psychology user behind the scenes who only presents what he wants us to believe in on the outside.

The target will often be young and exude personality traits that are consistent with someone who is open and friendly and likely to engage with a stranger. In this example, we are looking at the dark psychology user who is planning to approach a complete stranger in a public place with the hopes that he can develop some kind of connection that will open the door to more interactions. You might think that one of the key ingredients to a plan like this is that the practitioner has to be really attractive. But the truth is that men can impress and charm other people without necessarily being the most attractive man in the room. If he's got the right preparations and knowledge in place, a man can be very charming without being devastatingly handsome, though this factor would certainly not hurt.

Different women are attracted to different types of personalities, and the practitioner who is aiming to charm a woman must pick up on these desired traits rather quickly into the interaction or personify them based on information he has gathered about her past and what type of men she likes. Keep in mind that the tables can easily be turned here where we are talking about a woman who is using dark psychology to seduce a man, though the tactics there will work in a woman's favor as the guide to most men's immediate attraction is purely physical. A man looking to seduce a woman can be a little trickier, so this is why we are looking at the process from this angle.

First impressions involve what most people view as superficial aspects of a person. When the man approaches his target, he will be dressed in a way that conveys to the target what he wants her to see. Is he a busy professional who was stopped in his tracks and just had to say hello? If so, he might be wearing a business casual ensemble with some pricey-looking accessories. Perhaps he is a sporty type and is wearing something casual but made to move in. This could be the route he would take if he wanted to catch while she was out for a job or a long walk. Perhaps he wants to look younger and adopts more of a gently tussled, boho kind of style to mirror the target's style, etc. His appearance will play into this first encounter and the impression he makes on his target, but then he has to open his mouth.

His approach is careful to be non-threatening and casual. He doesn't want to scare her away by approaching her with an obvious objective, say, of spouting off a pickup line then asking for a phone number. The best approach will happen if it appears the man just happens to be in the same place at the same time and is intrigued by the appearance of this attractive woman. He doesn't want to assume to steal away her time if she is not amenable to giving it away, and the approach itself might have to wait until a better time if he does not get a positive response right away. If it appears he is bothering her in any way, he will probably need to take a step back and try again another time, or else move on to a different target.

But if he is successful and approaches in a way that does not alarm the target, she will send him a positive signal, such as a smile or a greeting. The progression to seduction will depend a lot on how well the dark psychology practitioner reads the target and how well he responds in a way that is effective and positively reinforcing his selected persona. Those who are skilled in this area will be able to charm the woman rather quickly. He knows that women like to be listened to and to feel like the person cares about what she is saying. To play into this, the practitioner may throw all kinds of wonderful compliments and questions and interest at her in order to convey that he is not only listening but very interested in everything she has to say. This will create a sense of camaraderie, and the longer this can be maintained, the more the target will feel comfortable talking,

and eventually, she might even release details about her life that will further work toward the practitioner's goals.

What the user will look for in this situation are the little subtle cues that the target is interested in. Often, we, as human beings, give signals subconsciously without our immediate awareness, and we all have certain reactions that go off automatically when we are entertained or interested in a conversation. The more positive signals the target gives off, the more these are taken by the dark psychology practitioner as a go-ahead to move forward with the interaction and to turn on the charm as much as possible.

The goal of this first interaction is to secure a second interaction. This could be explicit with an outright invitation to hang out again in the future or for a date, or it could be another "coincidental" meeting at which both of these individuals run into each other, perhaps during a similar activity or set of circumstances as this first interaction. Each time the practitioner interacts with his target, the goal will be to increase the attraction that may have started when the two of them first met. The progression will look a lot like a dating situation, but the dark psychology user is using tactics that are covering up the truth of the motivations and goals underneath.

In another scenario, the practitioner may have the goal to get a girl to come home with him the same night. One of the most commonly used tools in this scenario is alcohol, with the intent of getting a girl drunk enough that she begins to make poor decisions and become overly trusting of complete strangers. When this situation is created, the dark psychology practitioner can simply make a few suggestions, and the woman may be convinced that she is in safe hands and can trust this man for a fun night without any commitments afterward.

Women can protect themselves from predatory behavior by being aware of the common tactics and warning signs when engaging with strangers. Some of the advice you've heard for years seem trite and obvious until a woman finds herself in a situation where her senses and thinking are clouded or distracted. It is also important to be on guard and aware of situations that may arise with close friends or family. Friends who attend a big party or go to a bar together should never abandon the group in favor of spending time with a man whom she just met that night, especially if she is drinking. Her friends should not allow this to happen, even if she insists, as the man in question seems unbelievably charming. The old saying about things that seem too good to be true usually are, is told over and over for a reason. If you suspect that someone you care about is under the influence of a master manipulator, it is important to talk with them about the possibility that they are being lied to as a means of getting something in return but not being straightforward. Don't be afraid to start that conversation if you believe there is a possibility that someone you care about is in danger. A lot of people may find the idea intimidating, or they hesitate because the friend might think they are overbearing or overstepping their bounds. It is always better to find yourself in disagreement with a friend than to find out that he or she has been abused or mistreated by someone they had thought they could trust or developed feelings for.

The truth is, when a practitioner of dark psychology is able to get past the seduction phase successfully, they will often continue the ruse because they enjoy playing with the control and trust they've won and enjoy basking in their prize. They may be using the individual as a way to make themselves look good, like a trophy, or they may be using this person as a means to some other end. The motivations behind such manipulation and abuse can vary widely, and the damage that can be done in the end should never be underestimated.

Chapter 7: The Dark Triad

The dark triad involves a set of deviant personalities, which are known very commonly to employ tactics of dark psychology as a regular, routine practice in their interactions with people. This is because what we consider normal interactive abilities and social skills are different in some way in regard to these three personality types, if they are there at all. The social skills set often developed by these personality types center around manipulation and the pretense of being normal and conveying normal human emotions. They find out very soon that this is absolutely necessary because they do not have the capacity for these particular feelings toward others. We often cite people in these three categories as being without feeling or without empathy for others. This means that they do not feel bad about hurting others or their pain when they are sad. They do not even feel empathy toward another person's feelings of anger and frustration. The members of this circle remain enigmas in a lot of respects, mostly because it is difficult for someone who is not a part of this circle to understand how someone could possibly function in a way that is devoid of human empathy and caring or true, honest love. These three personalities of the dark triad include the sociopath, the narcissist, and the Machiavellian personality type. We will take a look at each of these categories in more detail.

Sociopath

The sociopath is often confused with another category of deviant personalities, the psychopath. However, they are different in a few key ways.

The most commonly recognized difference between the sociopath and the psychopath is that the sociopath personality is developed after birth, while the psychopath is born with this particular deformity. Sociopaths endure experiences such as childhood trauma or abuse, or perhaps they learn non-empathy from role models or the people with whom they are brought up around. Whatever the examples, this behavior pattern and mindset are developed or learned through a process of living and experiences that involve triggers and formulations for the deviant personality type, while the psychopath is innate in the affected person at birth, including all that this personality involves. The sociopath and the psychopath can be very similar in nearly every other way that people are commonly familiar with. But the fact that the sociopathic personality is formed as a result of living and learned through experiences means that there is a lot of room for subtle changes and emotional nuance. The sociopath is not immune to feelings like empathy and guilt, though the threshold is quite high, and these feelings might be ignored in favor of continuing the hurtful behavior simply because the sociopath still places himself higher in

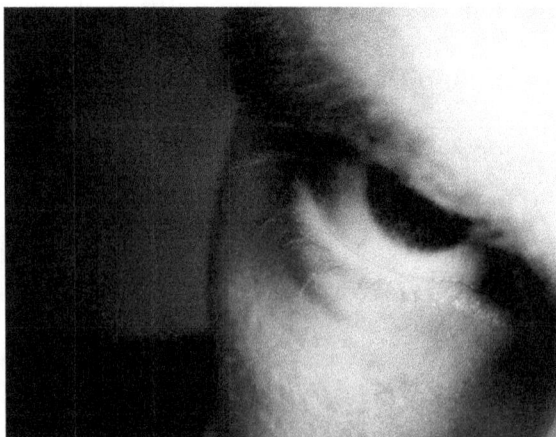

importance above other people. The psychopath, on the other hand, did not develop feelings of empathy or pick up on subtle changes in emotions through experience and learned behavior. They are simply not wired with the capacity to feel for others.

Sociopaths often develop skills related to dark psychology strategy out of the necessity to convince other people around them that they are "normal" in the sense of human compassion, empathy, romantic love, etc. To do this, they figure out what makes people tick and how to fool people. This develops in many different ways. Perhaps they had an adult figure at a young age who taught them through example how to lie and cheat and manipulate to get what they want. Perhaps they started to try things on a trial-and-error basis to figure out what works and what doesn't with different sorts of people. Or, perhaps they grabbed a few books and did some practical studying to understand the human brain and the psychology of emotions. However, they eventually get to a place where they have mastered some dark psychology skills, and they usually end up using people on a regular basis in their adult lives simply out of habit and necessity to continue living for the benefit of themselves.

Narcissist

The term narcissist is probably thrown around even more often than sociopath and psychopath and comes with its own set of connotations. The narcissist is often depicted as the well-dressed man with a deceptive smile and "affect" who goes around fooling people into doing things for him or giving him things under false pretenses. These "gifts" can be anything from money and donations to sex, power, influence, and admiration. The narcissist has an addiction to satisfying himself and his own needs and desires. He pursues fame and appreciation and praise and will do whatever is necessary to place himself above everyone else and then to gloat about it. The narcissist is also devoid of human emotions where it concerns other people. He does not love in a conventional way; he simply pretends to love another for the sake of being loved in return. It is all about him.

Narcissists develop as a response to life experience, how he is raised, or how he is treated by others. The narcissist is not born a narcissist like a psychopath is born a psychopath. However, while the sociopath may be able to recover some capacity for empathy, guilt, and compassion, it is rarely seen that a narcissist makes any degree of the same kind of recovery. In other words, once a narcissist, always a narcissist. Now, the narcissist may be very clever in that he could convince persons of interest that he has changed or seen the light or "come to Jesus" in this respect, but it is, most often, a complete lie in order to get some type of attention or praise. Again, manipulation and dark psychology are the narcissist's bread and butter, and when those skills start to develop, and the individual sees the fruits of his labor, it only gives the narcissist more fuel and motivation to continue and get better at these skills. They will use the skills on anybody and often target those who are emotionally vulnerable and naïve.

We talked earlier about the "long game" in which a practitioner of dark psychology invests months, years, and even decades into manipulating and controlling a single individual. This is most often associated with a spouse, partner, or business colleague. The possibilities here are countless in terms of what exactly the narcissist is aiming for, but we can be assured that it is something about personal gain in some form.

The tragedy among those who are fooled into believing a narcissist is someone he isn't is that the target who has fallen in love often falls into the trap of believing they can somehow "change" the narcissist through enough love and dedication. This is especially sad because it feeds perfectly into the narcissist's trap who only desires to keep the claws of attachment deeply ingrained in his target so that he can continue to siphon love, support, and affirmations for as long he wants. We discussed earlier a technique in which the target is strung along then pushed away, only to be brought back together and given satisfaction until the next time the practitioner pulls away. This technique cultivates a feeling of desperation in the target with just enough attention and occasional showers of affection that the target does not cut ties completely. This is an ideal situation for the narcissist who desires to pursue other interests without having to dedicate all of his energies on a single target. He may utilize an occasional form of communication in order to make sure his first target is still "waiting" on him while he very well could be exercising a whole new romantic situation with another vulnerable female.

The narcissist gets a lot of excitement and satisfaction from challenging himself and finding himself successful in manipulating those "hard to get" types. It is just another source for him to glean self-praise and admiration. He will also move against anyone else in his purview who tries to usurp what he has gained or exposes him to other people. He will also use any measures necessary to accomplish the removal of those obstacles. The great majority of serial killers fall under the category of the narcissist, among others, as they are obviously willing to do whatever needs to be done in order to satisfy their own desires. They do not feel guilt or shame in the same way that "neurotypical" human beings do, or else this sensation would override their desires, though they often insist, once caught, that they had felt remorse after killing.

Machiavellian

This component of dark triad personalities is named after an individual who espoused a work called *The Prince* that states that the necessity for proper and effective leadership is absolute in the sense that, essentially, "the ends justify the means." The leader must do what is necessary in order to enforce rules and maintain power. Nothing is off the table when it comes to making sure these needs are met and to eradicate any threat to that seat of power. His writings supported the use of force, fear, and harsh punishment as a means of making sure the populace remained under control and were discouraged from going against the leader's wishes and orders.

The Machiavellian personality is most closely associated with the personal accumulation of wealth. He is the miser sitting atop his mountain of gold while looking around at everyone else who lives without sufficient means even to live. He is also without much capacity to feel for other human beings. He does not look at the less fortunate and feel compelled to give some of his wealth; he is more likely to look at the penny or two in their possession and try to take them for himself.

Dark Psychology Tactics of the Dark Triad

The three components of the dark triad are centers for demonstrating the necessity to manipulate and use dark psychology tactics as a way to function in a world full of people who are different from you in a few very important ways. The lack of that which makes us feel like we can connect and use other people as support mechanisms for getting through life necessitates that those needs are fulfilled elsewhere. What exactly is it that the narcissist lives for, if not to connect with others or have a family to nurture and protect? The answer for all three of these personality types is that the self becomes a god at an early age, and everything the individuals do thereafter is, in effect, an act of worship to that god.

To illustrate, think of a devoutly religious follower who devotes a good amount of time to the study and worship of that god. Everything this believer does is pursued through the lens of doing what his god wants, and he follows the rules and regulations set before him in ancient religious texts as a sort of guide for how he is to live his life. If he feels called to go to a foreign country as part of a missionary trip, then he will do what he can to raise the money to support himself while he is away and take every opportunity to do what needs to be done there in the name of his god.

The personalities of the dark triad function in a similar way, only in that they themselves are the gods who they follow and worship. When a god calls for sacrifice, even if the sacrifice is another human being, history has shown that human beings are willing to offer this blood for the sake of satiating the desires of their gods. The narcissist, too, will sacrifice other people in the name of what is more important and the person in his life who is most deserving above all others—himself. The same line of thinking follows for the other components of the dark triad, each centering on his own specific obsessions and pursuits, none of them altruistic in nature but completely self-serving.

The problem for them is that to get what they want, they often need to go through other people. And this is where the necessity for dark psychology comes in. Not only will they often have a natural affinity for the skill, but they also find it fun to mess with people. They feel affirmed to look as if they have made a fool of others, which props themselves up as the smarter, superior being. They themselves would never consider that they could be susceptible to such manipulation, and

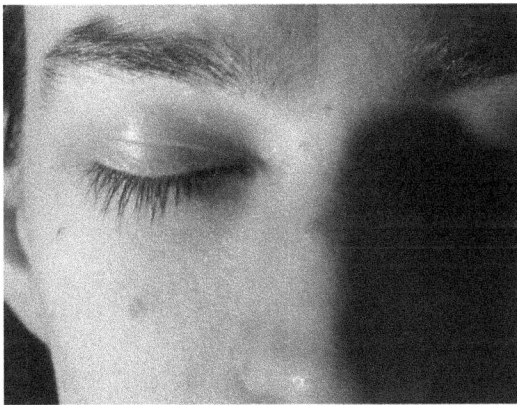

they are often immune to such strategies for the simple fact that they don't have those pesky emotional vulnerabilities that most other people share. They do not trust others but instead seek to get other people to trust them, love them, and admire them.

The easiest way to fool others in this regard is to closely observe and then emulate human behaviors that will make them appear as though they feel just as other people feel. They can make people fall in love with them, or they might exploit another's pity through deception in order to get a handout or some other type of free influence—whatever needs to be done.

One of the most fascinating and insidious characteristics of the members of the dark triad personality group is their capacity for denial when it comes to being challenged directly when they are caught in their schemes. In terms of gaslighting practices, when they are given clear evidence of their behavior and are asked to acknowledge their actions, they will simply disregard and deny without budging an inch. This is infinitely frustrating for the victims or the individuals trying to make sense of the dark triad's motivations and foundations for behavior. All we can do is stare at them in awe of how they can so readily disregard any and all attention to others and their concerns simply because they don't care; perhaps they are even bored.

The most painful experience in relation to dealing with individuals of the dark triad personality types is when that realization comes through, and you are unable to completely get rid of the feelings you've developed for this mask that has been hiding an insidious person. When the realization hits the victim, it is like having that person with whom they've been in a relationship suddenly disappear. It can feel as if the love of one's life has died, and there is just this demon in his/her place. If the target cannot come to terms with this realization and this unmasking of the truth, then she may try for years and years to get back that illusion of a relationship, even going so far as to live in denial herself. This is one of the most truly tragic results that can occur in a situation involving dark triad personalities and dark psychology.

But there are even more horrible ends to a situation in which a dark triad personality pursues a desire and stops at nothing to gain it. Murder, abuse, and other inconceivably horrible actions have been utilized in order to satisfy the simple, basic urges within them. That part of most of us which will stop us from doing such things for the sake of selfish pursuits is completely absent in these individuals, and their most basic urges and selfish desires often have free reign and influence over their behavior. It is a terrifyingly fascinating structure within these individuals that they can at once be harboring such animalistic and selfish natures while being perceived by other people as persons of high moral standing and poise. These traits make those on the spectrum of the dark triad personalities some of the most dangerous people on the planet.

Chapter 8: The Art of Deception and Mind Games

Harry Houdini was a famous entertainer and escape artist who mastered his craft at an early age and became known around the world at the turn of the 20th century for his risky public escapes and meeting challenges presented to him while a crowd of onlookers watched in amazement. Newspapers would advertise where he would be and what he was planning to do so that when he was ready to perform his stunts, there would be a massive crowd of people waiting for him. Most people today who recognize his name immediately associate him with the amazing escapes he performed, such as getting out of a straight jacket or escaping from chains while submerged underwater. What many don't know is that in the latter part of his career, he also became obsessed with the occult and the idea that one could talk to those who had passed away through rituals known as "seances." But he soon became angry about the appearance of scam artists whom he claimed were taking people's money and then faking the ritual through the use of cheap tricks that make customers believe they were actually reaching dead loved ones and relatives. It angered him so much that he took it upon himself to attend some of these events and expose the tricksters, catching them in the act, as he was familiar with the tricks they would use because he was an accomplished and well-studied magician who could spot what was going on. The routine would go something like this:

Houdini would attend one of these seances under the guise of having lost someone he loved. He would play the part well of a grieving husband and make up a story to support his claims. He would then sit down at a large table with other guests who were also there to try and communicate with lost loved ones. The seance would progress with a selection of tricks and techniques which would transform the atmosphere and play with the guests' perceptions of what was happening. Houdini would be able to spot these things, ranging from rigged lights and surfaces that would move on command or emit light seemingly from nowhere. Eerie sounds would float through the air, and the guests were told that it was the arrival of spirits, but Houdini knew that there were other people involved who were putting these things into action under the cover of dimmed lights, etc. He would stand up and abruptly interrupt the proceedings in order to expose what was going on. These events and Houdini's actions would be told through news stories, and he soon became well-known for his personal mission to expose frauds in this way. An interesting detail is that Houdini did actually believe in communication with those who had passed into the afterlife. He even talked with his wife about a secret phrase he would use should one of them pass so that they could communicate when one would try to reach the other. After Houdini died tragically following a stage performance, his wife tried for years and years to reach her husband using this secret phrase and utilizing every medium she could find, to no avail.

This example of the rigged seance is brought up here as a good illustration of how mind games can work together to form a completely altered reality in the minds of the victims. Let's begin with an examination of the target's initial mindset.

The seance practice targeted those individuals who had lost a loved one and wished desperately to communicate with them. They would have been in varying stages of the grief process, and anyone would pinpoint these individuals as being emotionally vulnerable. The intensity of certain emotions can drive human beings to do crazy things and to experience even more outlandish ideas and thought processes. The human mind actually has an incredible capacity and proclivity to do what it can to protect itself from pain, including emotional pain. When we get close to something hot, and we are in danger of being burned, our nerves send a signal to our brains in the form of increased pain as we get closer to the source. This tells us to get away from that source of danger immediately, and we often react physically even before our minds process what is going on. Anyone who has ever accidentally touched something burning hot can attest to this phenomenon.

We also have built-in mechanisms which are triggered when we are dealing with emotional pain. Depending on the intensity of emotions, the mind can trick us into believing something that isn't true—this is the case in those situations where someone is given tragic news, and their initial reaction is denial until they can wrap their minds around what is happening. We may also be prone to reaching out to far-fetched possibilities in the hopes of easing the intensity of the pain, which comes with loss, even so far as, say, reaching out to someone who promises that they can connect us with those lost loved ones.

The first use of dark psychology tactics appears in the form of the salesman who speaks to a potential customer—someone hurting emotionally as a result of a terrible loss. Here, the salesman listens intently with a sympathetic ear. He hears everything that the subject says and relays his feelings of empathy and condolences. This step is incredibly important for the manipulator because this is when he will begin to glean details and information that he will need to use later to support his ruse. He will listen to little details specific to the lost loved one. This tactic was often used as a way to personalize the experience and heighten the sense of believability during the seances themselves. He may pick up during this initial conversation that the customer's daughter was killed during a train accident, for example. She had been traveling with a pet dog and was wearing one of her favorite blue dresses, etc. People who are in the middle of a grieving process or who are going through some other type of emotional distress might be inclined to ramble as a way to relive and touch those experiences and those people who no longer exist in their lives. Talking about lost loved ones has a way of reinvigorating their memory and, in a way, brings them to life for a brief time as those memories are alive in the subject's mind and heart while she speaks. The target may not even realize that she is relinquishing these details but may be lost in reverie, to the dark psychology user's benefit.

The customers might then be brought into a specially prepared room. One of the key aspects of this deception is the ambiance of the room itself. The room would have been dimly lit, with a large table as the focus of the room. The individual who is supposed to be the conduit for the spirits to use for communication may wear a special outfit or something that signifies that they are a special component in this exercise. The room may be outfitted with lots of candles to enhance the other-worldly feeling of the environment and the customers' intentions.

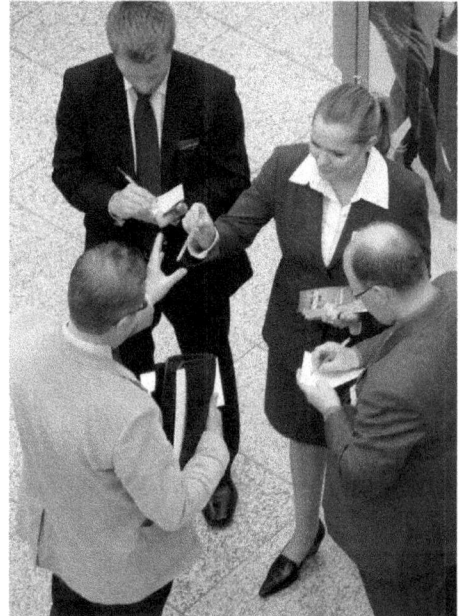

The customers all sit down at the table, usually a big circle, and then the next very important step to the ritual begins. The leader of the ritual speaks to the customers in an urgent, sincere tone that signifies the beginning of a very sacred and intense proceeding. The speaker uses aspects of character, such as tone of voice, eye contact, and intensity, to convey the weight of what is about to happen. As the targets listen to this proceeding, they begin to feel the passing of intensity, and this further heightens the environment's otherworldly effect. The mind does the rest in terms of solidifying that the targets are being thoroughly convinced of their situation and what is about to happen. Each subject is desperate for this situation to be real, and they do well in convincing themselves through hopes and wishes that they will soon be able to connect with those they desperately miss. At this point, their own minds are working against them in the form of denial as they dismiss any rational argument that may be trying to enter their minds regarding the validity of what they are experiencing. They make the decision to trust what these people are saying, and, once this happens, the door opens wide for continued deception and mind games.

The next step in the proceeding is for the actual ritual to begin. Effects designed to startle and amaze the targets are put into action according to a meticulously laid out plan. Things start to happen, which appear to be happening without anyone in the room having any influence on those actions. These would include things like candles being blown out, the table moving or rumbling objects placed on the table moving without anyone's volition, and other similar actions. Noises and eerie sounds that were designed to sound like they are coming from the beyond would also emanate at key points in the ritual's proceedings. As these phenomena happen, the subjects would be fed further proof that what they are experiencing is real as they continue to take what they are indeed real and valid. The mind processes only those things which prop up and substantiate what it has already decided to believe. At the same time, those minds would have immediately disregarded evidence that pointed to the contrary belief that all this was a ruse. For example, if someone were to accidentally step out of the shadows and into the customer's view from the table, the customer, having already solidified himself in his beliefs about the proceedings, would likely not even process that person's presence in their visual field.

Another common practice that served to help make the deceptions and tricks so convincing was to have the subjects hold each other's hands in clear view of each other, including the leader of the seance ritual. Doing this was evidence that these strange phenomena were not being enacted or influenced in any way by the ritual leader, so, as logic could enter the picture in these subjects' grieving and desperate minds, the only presence that could be enacting these phenomena were those present in the afterlife coming to talk to them.

The next component of the ritual lies in the acting skills of the ritual leader. She was presented as one through which the subjects' loved ones could reach out and speak to them. The level of the suspension of disbelief here is a vivid and potent reminder of how much our own minds can play a part in the deceptive mind games involved in dark psychology.

And this is where that information, gleaned earlier from each of the subjects, would come into play. The actor might start to act strangely, and she would completely change the tone and timbre of her voice in order to convey that she was being "taken over" by the spirits in the room. The actor would then begin addressing each subject under the guise of their lost loved ones. This might be played up as if the subject's loved ones were actively searching for the presence of their family or friend. The subject might then be prompted to reach out and say something like, "I'm here. I'm listening." The subjects would then be able to have brief conversations, and perhaps the actor would describe how the connection was a little cloudy, and she could only relay a few sentiments to their loved ones of their choosing. The actor might also say a few words through an altered voice that was meant to be believed as the voice of the lost loved one. Imagine being one of these poor people believing they were talking to their dead loved ones. The experience must have been mind-altering, and the impressions on the ritual would have lasted for a long time afterward, perhaps being one of the few things the subjects would cling to as sustenance for years to come.

The ritual would conclude according to a planned timeline of events. The subjects would not be allowed to simply say everything they wanted to or to have an hours-long conversation with their dead loved ones because the longer the ruse goes on, the higher the likelihood that something is going to trip the scammers up, or the customer might venture into unknown territory that they would not be able to play into. After the final escalation of the ritual, the mood and intensity are gradually brought down, as the spirits essentially "go back" to where they had come from, and the original demeanor and voice returns to the ritual leader. They dispel the illusion and are brought back to reality and left to ponder what has just happened to them. In the scammer's idea of a best-case scenario, the customers would come back, again and again, to speak to their loved ones, forming a continuous line of income that is graciously accepted.

Cold Reading

Cold reading refers to a dark psychology tactic that exploits a similar facet of human nature, which is the desire to believe what we want to believe and also to see patterns and connections where we desire to see them. Research has uncovered a tendency in human nature to personalize the information that actually applies to a broad spectrum of people. This is illustrated most clearly in the horoscope that you find online or used to find in newspapers, where there was a set of "readings" that people would apply to themselves based on their birthdays. The horoscopes would be written out for each individual month of the year and corresponded with each month's astrological sign. These "messages" and readings can be fascinating to people who are particularly susceptible to this phenomenological tendency to associate themselves with personal readings like this, which are, in fact, broadly applicable. If you go through and read not just your own month's readings but all of them, you would find that a lot of the other readings also find meaning in connection to your own life, simply because of the broad possibilities of interpretation and application present.

Cold readings follow the same principle and are generally applied in face-to-face interactions; only, the process in this situation is a progression rather than a static series of statements such as in a horoscope.

The cold reading begins with broad generalizes statements and progresses to individual personalization based on the subject's reactions. These reactions are relayed with not only words themselves but also with body language and micro-expressions or expressions that are so brief and minute that most people don't pick up on them unless someone is really looking for them. The practiced cold reader is one of these people and knows what to look for. These signals are important to notice because they will give the practitioner clues as to whether or not he is heading in the right direction. A negative micro-expression might signal that he is off and needs to switch gears, while a positive signal will tell him to keep going along the same track. Some of this is navigated through a series of questions in the form of trial and error. A tidbit of information is followed until the trail runs cold, and the reader must try something different.

Positive expressions and signals include things like wide-eyed expressions of amazement or of being startled, signifying that the reader has hit on a truth that the subject is surprised he knows about. Grinning and chuckling can be other positive tells in this context. Body language also plays a big role in cueing the reader on whether he is heading in the right direction or not, and we will discuss this facet in more detail in chapter 10.

As an example, let's examine the following conversation.

The subject is greeted and is smiling and excited about the prospect of cold reading. She might be a little skeptical, but she also thinks it is fun to try out. The reader will recognize this as a good subject simply because there is eagerness as well as a limited level of skepticism. She isn't completely against the idea that someone could cold read her, and this is the type of attitude that makes a good cold reading subject.

The reader might start with some broad statements and assumptions based on the subject's current mood and demeanor. "You've been having a pretty good day today." The subject smiles and giggles. "And you've been able to share some good times with people you love." More smiles, more positive reinforcement. "You've got a special someone here with you today." The subject looks suddenly embarrassed, signaling he's hit the jackpot. "Ah, maybe this person doesn't even realize he is the subject of your affections." At this point, there might be a reaction from someone in the crowd. From the surface, it seems as though the reader has simply read this female without her giving him any information. But the truth is, she has given him a great deal of information, even if she wasn't aware of it. This is the nature of dark psychology.

Chapter 9: What Is Brainwashing?

The term brainwashing has a long and interesting history of connotations and associations. Sometimes, the first thing people might think of is the appearance of brainwashing and mentions of the process in movies and TV, in which hyper-evil individuals use psychological and sometimes, super-human techniques to get another person or group of people to do their bidding. Much like the misconception of hypnosis as a way to turn people into robots, the idea that brainwashing is a process by which a person can be turned into a robot for use by some dominant entity is also false and grossly exaggerated.

Brainwashing refers to the manipulation of the mind through dark psychological strategies and fits snugly under the umbrella of several topics that we have already discussed. Tactics, such as gaslighting and cult-recruitment, all employ a level of brainwashing and varying degrees and forms of dark psychology. During the era of the Milgram experiment, researchers and the curious used the term to examine the phenomenon of a collection of seemingly intelligent and "normal" people who could enact such atrocities as was witnessed during the holocaust.

At the core of the brainwashing process is consistent repetition. We've discussed the process of gaslighting and how this effect manifests over time as the same untruths and deceptions are repeated and reinforced many times over a period of time. Brainwashing, too, takes time, as well as repetition and consistent reinforcement as a way to condition the brain either away from old habits or to form new ones in the way of new belief systems and paradigms. We can look at the Jonestown cult phenomenon as a good example of how this is done and can be done.

Jim Jones was an incredibly charismatic speaker. He was skilled with communicating with people, and he could impress upon them that he could lead them to a place of salvation and refuge from their pain and suffering, which took on as many forms as there were followers. His words were powerful, but he also used additional tactics to further cement his followers' belief in him through things like rigged "miracle" healings. This might sound familiar from our discussion of seances and the tactics used by scammers to solidify the witnesses' suspension of disbelief. Those who fell into the cult's mindset and belief system were also taken advantage of by recruiters playing on the individuals' fears, emotions, desires, and sources of pain. The promise of a way out of suffering is something that all of us have the capacity to be tempted by. And those of us who think we would be above such tactics, and would never buy into such ideas from a cult, could possibly have been prime targets for these recruiters simply based on their willful ignorance. No one is completely above human psychology, and all of us have emotions and pain that occupy our time and energy in an effort to find ways to alleviate those sources of suffering.

The point at which a potential victim is convinced to hesitate is the moment when the brainwashing process begins. If a person is able to shut down an interaction completely without giving in an inch, it is likely that the perpetrator will simply move on to an easier target, and we will outline exactly how this can be done in our chapter on best practices and defenses. But if the initial approach is successful, then the recruiter or another type of brainwasher has managed to find a thread of connectivity that they can then build upon to form a more solid foundation inside the target's mindset. To enact a process of brainwashing on a freethinking individual, who is not a prisoner, is an indicator that the dark psychology practitioner has developed his skills and has planned the interaction down to that last detail, as it is often difficult to get complete strangers to let you in, to this degree. Most people have a healthy level of boundaries around them and their minds, but that is why hitting on vulnerability is vital to the successful brainwashing attempt. For example, the person out on the street looking for a victim to brainwash is certainly going to go for the young girl crying on a bench, as opposed to the happy-go-lucky jogger smiling and humming to a happy tune. There is a need present with the young girl, and if the brainwasher can find a way to convince her that he can assuage that need in some way, then there is an opportunity to begin that repetitive reinforcement until the girl believes whatever it is he wants her to believe.

We form habits and break habits all throughout our lives. Sometimes, we have to put forth a great deal of effort to break a bad habit. Other times, we simply form new ones without even trying, based on experience and the influence of others. The mind is malleable in the sense that a person intent on brainwashing another person for whatever reason can see progress as long as he is able to reinforce the ideas through repetition. All it takes is for the door to open just a crack. Then the progression is just a matter of time, unless something drastic happens and, for whatever reason, the interactions are cut short between brainwashing and the victim. These repetitions could entail things like the presentation of evidence or repeated arguments that are framed in such a way as to seem believable and well-founded. The process can become more efficient if more people are involved in the reinforcement process. In other words, ten people arguing for the same beliefs is a lot more convincing than one lone person. When the brainwasher can employ more people into the ruse, then there is an element of peer pressure and the pressure to conform, which adds to the impact of the brainwashing process. This is something that certainly contributed to the followers' comfort level in the case of Jim Jones. The congregation of followers would regularly be surrounded by devout, passionate people, and the feeling in place must have been electrifying. Words spoken to the crowd in this context would have held a high level of intensity and an appearance

of gravity unlike what they would have experienced should the words have been

spoken on an individual level without the influence of others.

Chapter 10: The Importance of Body Language

Body language is one of the major components of many forms of dark psychology tactics. This is because body language is actually more prevalent in terms of communication between human beings than speech. The key is whether or not you know what to look for and how to interpret body language in various situations. Let's take a look at a few examples.

Body language is often discussed when we're talking about displays of power and dominance. We've talked about the use of dark psychology in efforts to take over a room as an alpha or to win over other people whom the practitioner wants to influence or establish rapport with. We have also talked about dark psychology in the context of dating and seduction, but in this chapter, we will take a deeper look at what is being said through nonverbal communication in these various situations.

Dominance

Body language is a key part of displaying dominance, no matter the context. When a person enters the room, people consciously and subconsciously make judgments about that person based on what they see, how they hold themselves, and other subtle cues of nonverbal communication.

Katie enters a room, and her head is held high. She is not staring at the floor; she is making eye contact with the people she passes by and offering a slight nod and a grin as a greeting. Her posture is erect, with her shoulder back, and her stride is wide and confident. There is a slight sway to her hips that seems natural, and her arms swing freely at her sides. She has yet to actually speak to anyone, but you can form a pretty clear picture of what this person looks like as she enters the room. What is her body language communicating to you?

If you can form some kind of picture based on this description, there should be several adjectives that might come to mind to describe her based on this nonverbal evidence. The first, as hinted at in the description, might be confidence. When someone holds themselves erect with their shoulders back, it tells people around her that she is not hiding from them and that she is confident enough to be on full display and to acknowledge and confront anyone she comes across, hence, the direct eye contact and brief greetings. And the higher the chin, the more the message moves across the confidence territory into the realm of dominance.

To assume and display dominance is to carry yourself in a way that does not connote fear or trepidation. The free swing of the arms and long strides suggests that she is not concerned with getting in anyone's way, and there is an unspoken expectation that people will get out of hers if need be.

Let us say Katie moves into one of the main offices, and there, she is awaited by a few powerful people who are meeting her for the first time. Now, we're ready for the handshake.

The handshake can actually say a lot more than most people know to look for, but it is common knowledge in the realm of power and money and politics that how you choose to shake someone's hand can be a strong signal to a person's attitude, as well as their perception of the person with whom they are shaking hands.

The way to signal a position of dominance involves shaking hands in a way that your hand is on top with the palm facing down. This places the other's hand in the subservient position or with the palm facing up. The grip and pressure which the person chooses to employ during a handshake also send a message about dominance. Politicians who are constantly being photographed as they shake hands with other leaders and political figures might make special efforts to convey dominance by shaking hands in this position and making sure their hand is sending a strong signal to those who know what it means.

Katie chooses, however, to shake hands in a balanced way that does not assume dominance but instead orients the position of hands as to be equal with palms facing each other. This sends a non-threatening message of balance and a willingness to cooperate with another. It is smart to avoid intimidating or using aggressive behaviors in a situation where you want to form a working relationship based on trust and mutual benefit. Katie also is careful to smile and directly address the people she is meeting with eye contact and attentiveness. This should echo back to the first instances in which we examined how attentiveness, listening, and active engagement with a speaker sends the signal that you are interested and invested in what the subject is saying.

From a broad point of view, we can say that Katie practices dominance and strong leadership when she is in front of her employees, and she likes to cultivate a balanced working relationship with higher-ups and colleagues of equal stature within the business.

There are certainly much more overt ways to assume dominance, such as outright aggression, and there are also very subtle, covert ways, such as in the instance of a young professional gradually taking over a room and winning the hearts of those whom he might later utilize to his advantage. The alpha then operates as the individual on top until another comes along who wants to take the position for himself, and the alpha is challenged.

Seduction

Seduction is another major category in which body language plays an especially vital role, both on the part of the person trying to seduce and his subject.

The reading of body language comes into play in this scenario as soon as the seducer makes his approach. From the moment the target acknowledges the seducer, she begins sending signals, which are both conscious and subconscious messages that will either reinforce the efficacy of the seducer's tactics or give him warning signs that his target is not as open to suggestion as he'd thought at first. Let's look at some examples.

The seducer approaches from behind the subject, who may be standing and listening to some music about to begin at a bar. When the approach happens, the target must turn her body to orient herself to the speaker if she is acknowledging the approach and willingness to engage. The seducer then examines how much of her body begins orienting toward him and how much she is responding by keeping her orientation pointed away from the seducer. If she fully engages and turns to meet and look the seducer head-on, this is a strong signal that the lady is amenable to the interaction and is a strong positive sign that the seducer has chosen the right target for his intentions. On the other hand, if the target remains facing toward the stage and/or does not move to orient any part of her body toward the seducer, then she is sending a strong signal that she is completely uninterested in an interaction at that moment. This could be motivated by a variety of different reasons, but the seducer would usually abandon his approach and perhaps try again a little later; otherwise, he may simply move on to a different target entirely.

The seducer pays attention to every movement and mannerism the target makes as he is engaging with her. The trick for successful interaction and seduction, however, is not to appear as if he is trying so hard to read her thoughts through her behaviors and nonverbal communication. An attempt at seduction, for example, which is accompanied by lots of staring at the target's body instead of her face, is certainly not going to go over well, as the seducer's intentions are all but being broadcast by his behavior and areas of attention.

The skilled seducer will be able to multitask as he listens to the target's words and pays attention to nonverbal cues as much as possible, without seeming like this is what he's doing. The seducer must come off as comfortable, friendly, and nonthreatening. The idea is to ignite some kind of attraction in whatever form he can. Once this is accomplished, he can begin playfully moving in as he exploits this newfound weakness. Positive body language cues that will often signal to the seducer that he is progressing well include smiling and giggling while keeping the body oriented toward the seducer. Women who are simply pretending to be comfortable and engage will often smile and giggle playfully, but the orientation of their bodies will give away their anxiety. The seducer would likely not move forward in this situation until he can inspire a little more comfort into the interaction. However, as the seducer persists, he also runs the risk of intensifying the anxiety, as the target may or may not be experiencing a gut instinct to stay away or get out of the situation. This can be a powerful tool on the part of the target if she is able to really pay attention and listen to her instincts when she feels something is a bit off.

As the seducer finds a target and is able to get some positive signals, he will use his own powers in the form of nonverbal communication to inspire attraction and interest. Flattery can be utilized in ways other than direct verbal communication. A seducer who wants to introduce just a bit of flirtation and sexual interest might let the target catch him looking briefly over her as he then quickly returns to face her. This tells her a lot of different things about the seducer, and if played correctly, it will work to the seducer's advantage if the signal comes off as playful and flirtatious without getting into creepy territory.

There is a balance to all of these behaviors and interactions, and the same methods may work differently based on the personality and demeanor of the target. This is why practiced seducers will zero in on specific types who more often respond positively to such advances.

Interest vs. Boredom

Sometimes, our body language broadcasts information about ourselves unintentionally, and this can be a fascinating thing to look for in public once you become familiar with some of the more common responses to human interaction.

Boredom is one of the things that can affect us in ways that we are unaware of until someone else points out directly the behavior or nonverbal message. Things like yawning almost subconsciously or eyes that wander off while someone is speaking are nonverbal communications that can tell a person that they're bored and uninterested in what you have to say. It can be quite embarrassing when a speaker knows what these signals mean and sees them going into action in the middle of a story or speech or monologue. Perhaps a perfect example of this happening is the high school classroom setting in which a room full of bored teenagers is leaning to the side with their heads in their hands. Sometimes, this behavior is intentional and meant to convey the feeling of boredom, but oftentimes, these behaviors just happen as a response to the boredom before the individual even knows he's doing anything. For the practitioner of dark psychology tactics, being able to tell when what he is saying to a target is having an effect or not through the skill of interpreting body language can be essential to the success of the tactic. If he can't pick up on this, then the interaction will probably simply amount to a great deal of wasted time.

On the flipside, feigning interest is something that most of us are very capable of doing, and we have all likely practiced this kind of "white lie" in our lives at some point. We've all been at a party and had to listen to a person's story that was not particularly interesting, but you didn't want to be impolite, so you feigned interest. Can you think of some common nonverbal cues to signal to a person that you are interested in what they are saying?

The first one that most people think of, and which is probably the most important, is eye contact. Making eye contact while a person is speaking to you is one of the clearest ways you can convey interest and respect. If your eyes are wandering all over the place, the speaker is likely to pick up on the fact that he or she is not holding your interest. Smiling, nodding, and responding to questions while interjecting comments to reinforce that you are listening and processing what is being said are other common ways to relay that you are actively engaged in the interaction.

Chapter 11: Best Practices and Defenses

Now that you have a much clearer idea of the different types and practices of dark psychology practitioners, we'd like to provide you with a brief list of tips for you to incorporate into your arsenal. This would allow you to be always on guard should a situation arise in which you might be encountering dark psychology in your own life. Spread these tips around to the people who are close to you so that you will not only help defend yourself but you will also protect those you care about and love. Erring on the side of caution is always preferable when finding yourself in a dangerous and confusing situation in which dark psychology is being used.

Trust Is a Commodity to Be Earned—Not Freely Given

Dark Psychology users often use the manipulation of emotions to bypass the guards we usually have up to help us discern between someone we can trust and someone we have no reason to trust yet. Yes, when someone who we don't know asks for help, it is often kind and generous to offer a helping hand, even if you don't know the person well. But there are certain situations when this behavior is inadvisable simply because of the possibility that the person asking for help does not have good intentions. One factor to pay attention to is the time of day or night when someone approaches you for help and whether or not the area is lit and in a public area. If you are out at night and there are no a lot of people around, then someone coming up to you and trying to get you to follow them somewhere should be a huge red flag. This person may be sincere, but he may also not be a good person. It would be preferable for you to feel safe and protect yourself by potentially leaving a person to deal with a flat tire on his car.

Don't Drink Alone

We're talking about being out at a party or at a bar as opposed to a nice glass of wine while you binge on Netflix at home. Never go out into a public setting alone where it would be easy for someone with bad intentions to take notice that you are alone and drinking. If you are somewhere waiting for company, be wary of anyone who tries to approach you and convince you to go somewhere while you are by yourself enjoying a drink.

Don't Be Afraid to Disengage

Most of us recognize that disengaging from interaction in the middle of a conversation is probably going to come off as pretty rude, but you should never discount a bad feeling about a situation just because you are afraid of being rude or impolite. Explain that you don't feel right about the interaction, or if you feel the need to do it, make up an excuse to get out of the situation quickly and leave. Call someone right away if you feel you need some backup or an escort home. If you are somewhere without a lot of people around, move toward a public area where there will be other people to ask for support if you feel the need.

Have a Panic Button

There are lots of gadgets and apps out there which offer discreet means of communicating with someone of your choosing should you find yourself in a situation you can't easily get out of without some help. If you are out by yourself for a walk or a jog or in a public place but are approached by someone who is a little aggressive in his tactics, you can simply press a button or open an app without the person noticing to let someone you trust know that you would like some help to get out of your situation. In today's modern world, it is highly advisable that you do your best not to be out and about without a way of communicating with people you trust in case anything comes up or happens unexpectedly.

Call Them Out

This defense may not be the most preferable for certain personalities, but for those of you who have no trouble speaking your mind and letting someone know when they are wasting your time, don't be afraid to call out a person who is trying to manipulate you and let them know you are on to their schemes. If the setting is public, go ahead and raise your voice a bit so that others can hear you. It may just serve as a warning to other potential targets in the area, and the practitioner will

likely feel embarrassed or feel the need to flee the scene, as his perfect cover has been blown.

Continue Your Study and Research of Dark Psychology Tactics

One of the best actions you can take as you guard yourself against future dark psychology tactics is to continue educating yourself on the myriad ways that dark psychology can manifest in day-to-day interactions and settings. These users are always trying to be creative, coming up with new and more insidious ways to get under people's skin for their own benefit and exploitation. The more you familiarize yourself with the possibilities, the better prepared you will be when a situation comes up.

Spread the Word

The knowledge and understanding you've gained from reading this book is something that could very well save you from a devastating situation in the future, which you would never see coming until it's too late. Letting others know about what you've learned and sharing the skills and tools explained in this book will serve to benefit others in the same way. If you know someone who has been the victim of dark psychology in some way, you know that this can have a devastating effect that often lasts for the rest of the victim's life. Emotional trauma and manipulation can be some of the most painful and insidious tactics a practitioner of dark psychology can use on another human being, so spending some time not only to educate yourself but also to educate others can be a really important way to save a person from this potential harm. Don't be afraid to talk to someone candidly if you feel there is someone in their life who is harming them in any of these ways. The human mind can often deceive itself through denial, and sometimes, it takes input from another rational mind to bring these individuals out of this dark place. It's worth the risk of being called nosy when you are legitimately afraid for another person's safety, especially if that person is someone who is special to you, like a close friend, partner, or family member.

On the same token, it is important to remember that you have placed your trust in these people for a good reason and that you may not have all the facts on which to base your assumptions. Calling people out as practitioners of dark psychology can be a serious accusation and should not be taken lightly. Have a serious and heartfelt discussion with those you trust in order to understand the situation more fully and to make rational decisions about what you should and should not do to help out those you care about.

In some situations, the scenario might involve someone you do not know. There are avenues through which you can report suspicious behavior anonymously should you suspect that someone nearby is being manipulated or exploited in some way. Again, if you've got alarms going off in your brain about a potential predator, try to get past those uneasy feelings of anxiety in order to step in and check on the person whom you are worried about. You just might be the catalyst for saving someone from a lot of heartache and pain, and you may even be responsible for saving someone's life. These outcomes should be at the forefront of your mind in a situation where you feel uncomfortable. Coming off as rude or impolite is a very low price to pay compared to shrugging those feelings off and letting an innocent person walk into a potentially dangerous situation.

Conclusion

Thank you for making it to the end of *Dark Psychology 101 2021: Understanding the Techniques of Covert Manipulation, Mind Control, Influence, and Persuasion*. Let us hope it was informative and able to provide you with all the tools you need to achieve your goals, whatever they may be.

After having completed this book, you will find yourself well on your way to being a part of a population that has acted in their own interest in terms of defending against users of dark psychology. Those who seek to use these tactics against others will not always look the part, and these particular individuals are the most dangerous because they are difficult to differentiate from others with normal and benevolent intentions. For this reason, using the knowledge and educating yourself on the techniques of dark psychology is a powerful tool to use to ensure that you are not caught in a situation where you've accidentally let your guard down in response to a manipulative technique. Knowing you are a human being just like everyone else and not above being manipulated is one of the key steps toward becoming impenetrable when it comes to aggressive dark psychology techniques.

You have familiarized yourself with common scenarios and tactics used by malicious dark psychology users, and you've understood the differences between the dark triad personality types. You also have a much clearer understanding of how your body language communicates things, which you may not have been cognizant of the past before reading this book. You can use this information not only as a defense against dark psychology users but also as a way to probe and gauge whether or not the people you interact with on a daily basis are sincere or simply trying to deceive those around them.

People are not always who they appear to be, and it is important that this message is ingrained into the minds of people from all walks of life and lifestyles. No one is off-limits when it comes to dark psychology, and you are now familiar with the idea that dark psychology is being used every day on a wide scale by people who do not necessarily have bad intentions and who are not actively trying to deceive. Sometimes, emotional reactions and demeanors can influence our behaviors in ways we do not understand unless we've done the research and practiced awareness of ourselves and our actions on a daily basis. Do a favor for those you love and trust by reaching out and sharing with them the knowledge you've gleaned from this book.

Finally, if you found this book useful in any way, a review on Amazon is always appreciated!